D1026022

MAKE YOUR OWN
SODA

MAKE YOUR

SO

Syrup Recipes for All-Natural Pop,

OWN
DA

Floats, Cocktails, and More

ANTON NOCITO FOUNDER OF P&H SODA CO.
WITH LYNN MARIE HULSMAN

 CLARKSON POTTER/PUBLISHERS
NEW YORK

Published in the United States by
Clarkson Potter/Publishers, an imprint of
the Crown Publishing Group, a division
of Random House, Inc., New York.
www.crownpublishing.com
www.clarksonpotter.com

CLARKSON POTTER is a trademark and
POTTER with colophon is a registered
trademark of Random House, Inc.

Library of Congress Cataloging-in-
Publication Data
Nocito, Anton.
   Make your own soda / Anton Nocito
with Lynn Marie Hulsman.—First
Edition.
      p.   cm
   Includes index.
   1. Carbonated beverages.   2. Syrups.
I. Title.
   TP630.N63 2013
   641.87′5—dc23
   2012018853

ISBN 978-0-770-43355-0
eISBN 978-0-7704-3356-7

Printed in China

Design by Stephanie Huntwork
Cover design by Stephanie Huntwork
Cover photographs by Alexandra
Grablewski

10   9   8   7   6   5   4   3   2   1

First Edition

This book is dedicated to my wife, Erica, and my son, Aidan

CONTENTS

INTRODUCTION

I'm a small-batch soda artisan on a mission. I want America to enjoy satisfying, all-natural sodas with flavors so sensational that one taste will blow your mind. No preservatives, no corn syrup, no artificial colors. I founded P&H Soda Co. on the idea that people want to travel back to a simpler time, when the seltzer man delivered to your home, a movie cost pocket change, and enjoying a soda was a way for people of all ages to kick back and celebrate.

In soda's early days, in the nineteenth century, a glassful was a tonic for what ailed you. It was used as a health food, in many ways. People would blend seltzer with herbs, fruits, and other natural flavors into a delicious, refreshing drink. But over the years, as big business took over, soda became a different thing altogether: chemicals swimming in sugar water, too-sweet fake flavors, guzzled down with no thought. But now—with increased interest in taking foods back to a simpler, fresher, more natural state—I'm taking soda back.

Some of my fondest memories are of going to Rumplemeyer's—an ice cream parlor that used to be on Central Park South, in Manhattan—with my dad and brother before a ballet or a Broadway show. We'd get so excited to indulge in a scoop of ice cream with a triangular *pizzele*-style cookie perched at the edge or to dig a long silver spoon into a tall glass to scoop out the first frothy mouthful of a creamy, bubbly ice cream soda. Deciding on my soda flavor was exquisite torture. The waiter would stand patiently by while I considered wild combos like pistachio ice cream with strawberry syrup, or orange sherbet with cherry syrup. More often than not, I chose the classic black and white, bubbling with rich chocolate and fragrant vanilla. I'd alternate between slurping the chocolatey beverage through my straw and digging into the melty vanilla scoop floating and bobbing in my glass. And I remember sitting at a soda-fountain counter with my grandpa Anthony, a jokester with a legendary sweet tooth. We'd sip on sodas while watching the ritual of the soda jerk pulling the gleaming silver handles, pouring syrups into fluted glasses with all the flair of a serious mixologist.

Soda is so much more than just cola, lemon-lime, and orange. This book shares inspired flavors like Coffee Syrup (page 62), with its rich-roasted smoky smoothness; Concord Grape Syrup (page 43), which explodes in the mouth with ripe, rich fruit; and fresh Lemon Verbena Syrup (page 40), with a clean herbal edge that could cut glass. With these recipes, you'll have your family and guests rethinking carbonated beverages.

FOUNTAIN FACT

The use of the term "soda water" first occurred in 1798, probably referring to natural mineral water. But it wasn't until 1810 that a patent was filed for a method of making the fizzy stuff artificially.

The other great thing about making your own soda syrups is how easy they are and how many different kinds of drinks and treats you can make using them. Homemade soda syrups are basic infusions, meaning you steep fruits, herbs, aromatics (like rose petals), or other ingredients in a simple syrup. Then, you just stir it into basic carbonated water, and you have a fresh soda! Add some ice cream to that soda, and you have a unique ice cream float (see page 102). Or you can use the syrups to flavor hot beverages (see page 133) and cocktails (see page 117). For those who remember going to real soda fountains, where a soda jerk would make to order a classic phosphate or lactart, I've included notes

SHOW NO FEAR!

"Fear nothing!" is one thing I stress to the home cooks in my kitchen classroom. Some of the greatest accomplishments come to us through the gift of mistakes. No one ever succeeded by trying not to fail. Experiment. What's the worst that can happen? So you take a sip of some crazy concoction like rosewater and pink peppercorn soda with a dash of spruce oil and you decide it's not for you. No big deal: it's cooking, not brain surgery. Try to take something away from the batches that aren't grand slams, and notice what you learn about texture, balance, and taste.

about how to re-create those familiar flavors—and I've shared my tried-and-true method for the most authentic egg cream. Finally, all along the way, I'll share interesting facts about soda and soda fountains.

We're a nation of soda drinkers. Call it soda, pop, soft drink, tonic, or "coke," we have a love affair with fizzy beverages. I hope that you'll be inspired by how easy and delicious homemade sodas are, and what a treat real soda can be. With these recipes, you can make Cream Soda (page 63) that tastes of nothing but caramelized sugar and the most aromatic vanilla; Hibiscus Syrup (page 70) that's the stuff of dreams, a jewel-toned syrup born of actual blooms, equally at home in cold seltzer or a glass of Champagne; and Ginger Syrup (page 27) with a peppery bite that will perk you right up.

Making your own soda, with the best of the best ingredients, really is easy when you use the simple techniques and suggestions found in this book. It's smart, it's economical, and it lets you decide the flavors and sweetness levels that are right for you. I'm glad you're on board for this exciting soda revolution!

MATERIA PRIMA: SIMPLY THE BEST

Aristotle said, "The whole is greater than the sum of its parts." And I agree, partly. The sodas and drinks I serve are phenomenal. Pure pleasure in a glass, they're an amazing treat. But they owe their greatness to their ingredients, which I am passionate about. I like to know where things come from and how they were cared for before they came to me. No sad, subpar, or out-of-season foods are allowed into my pots, bowls, or bottles.

Materia Prima, poetically translated, means "essence above all." That's the guiding principle for all I do. I like things to be easy to understand. When you look at a P&H Soda label, you'll see it says fresh, organic ginger, and organic spices—and you know what it is. You know what's in there. With the recipes in this book, you can make sodas that are this simple—this fresh and real—too.

GETTING STARTED

THE TOOLS OF THE TRADE

Investing in a few basic tools will save you time and labor. For most of the drinks in this book, the following tools are all you need to make the job a breeze. Chances are, you probably already own most of them.

VEGETABLE PEELER: I don't know why we leave fruit out of the name of this handy gadget, but one tool will do the job for vegetables and fruits alike. Choose a top-mounted or side-mounted blade on a handle, or the rotating apple or potato peeler that removes the skin in one long spiral.

MICROPLANE ZESTER: Sometimes called a Microplane grater, the common denominator for this useful tool is very small holes coupled with a very sharp surface.

POTATO MASHER: Nylon or metal, a flat circle with holes or a zigzag of loops, the effect is the same—nicely smashed ingredients. I like to use my grand-mother's, which is heavy and sturdy.

BLENDER/ IMMERSION BLENDER: A regular blender with a glass or plastic carafe is probably all any home cook needs. An immersion, or "stick," blender is nice when you want to limit mess and keep your ingredients in one container.

COCKTAIL SHAKER: The three most common types of cocktail shaker are the Boston Shaker, the Cobbler Shaker, and the French Shaker. For the Boston, a metal top is ed in conjunction with a glass or plastic cup, and a separate strainer is necessary. The Cobbler is a three-piece apparatus with the strainer built in and a cap that doubles as a jigger measure. The French is a simple model with a metal top and bottom and needs a separate strainer. In a pinch, you can always use a plastic cup and glasses of two different sizes, each with a mouth wider than its base, and strain through a fine-mesh strainer.

FINE-MESH STRAINER: A regular, bowl-shaped fine-mesh strainer on a handle is perfect for straining syrups that have been steeped with spices or fruits.

CHEESECLOTH/ COFFEE FILTERS: Cheesecloth is inexpensive and a handy thing to keep in your kitchen. Coffee filters will also work well when straining syrups that have fine sediment to extract.

SODA SIPHON OR OTHER HOME CARBONATING DEVICE: If you're keen on carbonating your own water, there are plenty of tools to get the job done. You can use the old-fashioned glass model you inherited from your great-aunt or picked up at an antiques mall, or one of the snazzy new types that use canisters delivered to your door. Bottled seltzer from the supermarket works perfectly well, too.

A CARBONATION PRIMER

Carbonated water—water in which pressurized carbon dioxide has been dissolved—goes by many nicknames: sparkling water, club soda, bubble water, two cents plain, fizzy water, soda water, mineral water, and even seltzer, a proprietary eponym linked to a German town boasting natural mineral springs, after which Alka-Seltzer was also named.

For home use, the "aerosol" bottle, an early soda siphon, was introduced in France, and it changed the way people drank hard spirits, allowing them to lighten up a glass of booze, making drinking more socially acceptable, especially for the ladies. The Victorian English followed with their invention of the gasogene, a blown-glass bottle made up of two globes on top of one another, encased in wire mesh or woven twine, as they had a tendency to explode.

In Europe, chemists invented and perfected methods of imitating naturally carbonated water by infusing it with sulfuric acid and chalk, allowing for large amounts to be produced commercially. The demand was high, as belief in its health-giving properties was widespread. Europeans trotted off to Spa in Belgium, Vichy in France, and Baden-Baden in Germany to "take the waters." That idea translated to the United States, making places like New York's Saratoga Springs and Arkansas's Hot Springs popular vacation destinations.

Now a mainstream drink, seltzer is readily available in restaurants, where it is dispensed from large tanks hidden behind the bar, and easily purchased in recyclable bottles from supermarkets. There are even great devices on the market for producing your own carbonated water at home. The most popular is the SodaStream, which very quickly and effortlessly carbonates a single bottle of cold water at a time.

FOUNTAIN FACT

In 1676, the Compagnie de Limonadiers of Paris produced the first cited (noncarbonated) soft drinks. An all-natural drink made with water, lemon juice, and honey, it was sold by the cup from tanks carried on vendors' backs.

BUYING THE BEST PRODUCE

Simply put, the better the produce, the better the soda. Using what's in season just makes sense—produce is not only at its best when it's growing with the rhythm of the seasons, but also at its most plentiful, and therefore cheapest.

Here are a few suggestions for what to buy when. This is by no means an exhaustive list, as what's truly seasonal will vary from place to place, depending on where you call home. The surest way to find what's seasonal is to ask the local growers themselves, as they stand at market stalls in front of what they recently plucked from a tree or pulled from the ground. Your supermarket's produce manager can also steer you in the right direction.

JANUARY: apples, grapefruits, kiwi, kumquats, Meyer lemons, Minneola tangelos, oranges, pomegranates, rose hips, Seville oranges, tangerines

FEBRUARY: apples, clementines, oranges, pomegranates, Seville oranges, tangerines

MARCH: apples, clementines, mangoes, oranges, tangerines

APRIL: apples, edible flowers, lemongrass, mangoes, tangerines

MAY: apples, blackberries, edible flowers, lemon verbena, lemongrass, mangoes, mint, parsley

JUNE: apples, apricots, bananas, basil, blackberries, blueberries, boysenberries, cherries, currants, edible flowers, huckleberries, lemon verbena, lemongrass, mangoes, mint, nectarines, peaches, raspberries, sour cherries, strawberries

JULY: apples, apricots, bananas, basil, blackberries, blueberries, boysenberries, cherries, currants, edible flowers, figs, huckleberries, lemongrass, mangoes, marionberries, mint, nectarines, peaches, raspberries, strawberries

AUGUST: apples, apricots, bananas, basil, blackberries, blueberries, boysenberries, chiles, Concord grapes, currants, edible flowers, elderberries, fennel, figs, finger limes (caviar limes), grapes, huckleberries, lemongrass, mangoes, melons, mint, nectarines, peaches, pears, plums, raspberries, sumac, strawberries, watermelon

SEPTEMBER: apples, asian pears, bananas, basil, blackberries, blueberries, chiles, Concord grapes, cranberries, edible flowers, elderberries, fennel, finger limes (caviar limes), grapes, huckleberries, kiwi, lemon verbena, lemongrass, mangoes, melons, mint, nectarines, pears, plums, sumac, watermelon

OCTOBER: apples, asian pears, bananas, basil, Concord grapes, cranberries limes), grapes, kiwi, lemon verbena, lemongrass, mint, oranges, parsley, pears, persimmons, pomegranates, quinces, tangerines

NOVEMBER: apples, asian pears, basil, cranberries, finger limes (caviar limes), kiwi, mint, oranges, pears, persimmons, pomegranates, rose hips, tangerines

DECEMBER: apples, mint, oranges, pears, persimmons, pomegranates, rose hips, Seville oranges, tangerines

MIXING A BALANCED SODA: SWEET AND SOUR FLAVORS

The best sodas have a great balance of sweetness and sourness. Understanding the ingredients that add sweet and sour will help you learn how to craft the flavor you're looking for.

Everyone's palate is different, and you can tweak your soda's sweetness and sourness to the exact note for you. On the sweet side, if you want to add a creaminess to your soda, honey may be to your taste. For a lingering sweetness that stays on the tongue, like the kind you get with a bottled Malta, give sorghum a try. For a clean, dry finish with an herbal freshness, stevia will do the trick. If you want more tartness, up the citrus quotient with lemon or lime juice. For a drink with the dry quality of ginger ale, squeeze in a couple of drops of lactic acid. Here's a basic summary to demystify some of the most common elements used to perfectly balance your soda.

Sweet

In the United States, our taste buds have been skewed to crave heavy sweetness, since lots of processed goods contain added corn syrup and white sugar. I think of soda as a sweet treat, and I don't always love the cloying sweetness of an artificial-tasting soda. Sugar is the first ingredient we think of as a sweetener. Other great sweeteners include:

MAPLE SYRUP: Made from the sap of the sugar maple, red maple, or black maple tree, it is classified into three grades, with several color classes. With a higher concentration of minerals than honey, maple syrup of any grade or class has an earthiness that cuts through the sweetness. The flavor ranges from delicate in the Grade A Light Amber variety, to almost buttery-sweet in the Grade A Light, to more bitter, with coffee undertones in the Grade A Dark Amber, to a dark honey, grassy maple flavor in the Grade B. In general, I recommend the lighter maple syrups for pale-colored soda syrups and the Grade A or B dark maple syrups for soda-syrup ingredients that can hold up to the stronger flavorings.

MAPLE SUGAR: The solid by-product of the process of manufacturing maple syrup and maple taffy, maple sugar is hard to make, as it's very easy to burn at the high temperatures needed to produce it. It's about twice as sweet as white granulated sugar, and can be thought of and used like natural cane sugar. Once found only in the northeastern United States or from the catalogs of sugar shacks, this sweetener is gaining popularity with the natural-foods crowd and is showing up in gourmet markets, specialty stores, and natural-foods markets.

HONEY: Richer than white sugar, it comes in many grades. The region where it was produced affects the flavor, as the bees that make it have access to varying kinds of flowers, and the color and potency can vary wildly. In general, use paler and more delicate honeys with less bold soda-syrup ingredients and the dark, rich honeys with fruits and herbs that can stand up to them.

SORGHUM: Sorghum is a traditional sweetener that comes from a cereal crop that thrives in harsh environments. Often used in the Deep South of the United States, this sweetener is golden in color and tastes a bit like molasses, but is sweeter, milder, and doesn't have the mineral aftertaste. It has an herbal lightness similar to that of wild honey.

AGAVE: Produced from a succulent plant, this super-sweet syrup is all-natural and dissolves easily in cold liquids, making it an ideal beverage sweetener. Think of it like honey without the strong flavor.

COCONUT SUGAR: With a large grain and slightly tropical flavor, coconut sugar should be used only when a distinct taste is desired, as it adds depth and a creamy, nutty flavor, as well as sweetness, to your recipe.

STEVIA: A lot of people like this natural, low- or no-calorie sweetener that's available in both liquid and powdered form. Derived from a shrub in the sunflower family, it takes longer to perceive its taste than sugar and is longer lasting. Some people notice a licorice-like aftertaste if a lot is used.

Sour

People love the taste of sourness in beverages, especially when it cuts through pure sugary sweetness. Delicious commercial sour drinks include Schweppes Lemon Sour, Apple Slice, and plain old club soda. Even Diet Coke devotees like to cut the sweet with a lemon wedge served on the edge of the icy glass in restaurants. It's easy to brighten sodas by adding an acidic sourness. Here's a list of common ingredients that impart a sour flavor:

LEMON JUICE: Nice and tart in flavor, often added to sweetened tea to balance the sweetness.

LIME JUICE: Similar to lemon juice, lime juice is sweeter, and many people think of it as a more tropical flavor.

VINEGAR: I agree that it's not the sexiest ingredient in your kitchen cabinet, but vinegar is an inexpensive, old-fashioned way to add a bit of pucker to your drinks. Its acidic taste offers a less fruity alternative to the traditional lemon and lime of many sour drinks.

Early settlers and farmhands loved to drink shrubs—a vinegar-based soft drink, usually made with cooked fruit—as a cooling beverage during summer days spent in the hot sun, doing hard labor. Sharp and pungent, there is no mistaking the distinctive vinegar flavor and it cuts through sweetness like a knife. With the different varieties, including apple, red wine, white wine, rice, sherry, and malt, you can try lighter or richer vinegars with different soda ingredients to find your favorite combo.

ACID PHOSPHATE: This chemical compound is partially neutralized phosphoric acid. Pure phosphoric acid has gotten a bad reputation in the natural community since it's very inexpensive to produce and is widely used in commercial soft drinks. Acid phosphate isn't as pure as citric acid and lactic acid (or vinegar and citrus juice, for that matter), but it is great when you want a sour note without adding a new flavor. It's less tart than citric acid, and it offers a nice tingle. That quality was sought after by early soda jerks in an attempt to replicate natural mineral waters, was a base for early flavored sodas made in the home, and later was added to bottled Victorian beverages. I like this acid best with darker, richer syrup flavors like Concord Grape Syrup (page 43) and Sour Cherry Syrup (page 32). You can purchase acid phosphate from Darcy O'Neil's Art of Drink website (see Sources, page 141), and from other Internet sites and wholesalers.

CITRIC ACID SOLUTION: This very weak organic acid is ideal for brightening a drink without adding the flavor of lemon juice or vinegar. You can purchase citric acid (sour salt) on the Internet and through home-brewing suppliers, and make your own solution (see below). You can also find premixed solutions in different concentrations from specialty companies through the Internet.

LACTIC ACID: This acid occurs naturally and is refined from sour milk. The taste is reminiscent of something fermented, and has an alkaline quality like that of grapefruit. Lactic acid is the best tart additive to use with lighter-colored soda syrups like ginger and pineapple if you want an alternative to traditional citrus juices. Lactic acid can be found at craft-brew suppliers, at wholesale beverage-making companies on the Internet, or on Darcy O'Neil's Art of Drink website (see Sources, page 141).

MAKE CITRIC ACID SOLUTION AT HOME

To make ½ cup of citric acid solution, stir 1 teaspoon of citric acid into ½ cup of warm water until the citric acid is dissolved. Store in the refrigerator in a covered glass container for up to 14 days.

A WORD ABOUT SUGAR

I like using the highest grade of organic sugar I can find. Many supermarkets and health-food stores carry organic sugar in many forms, such as in large crystals or as granulated sugar, caster sugar, and superfine sugar. In some recipes, I prefer to use caster sugar because it dissolves easily. Make your own fine-grind sugar by buzzing larger-grained varieties in your (very dry!) blender or food processor.

Don't be fooled by confectioners' sugar. Some say it melts quickly and easily because it's a powder, but it has added cornstarch. All in all, it doesn't work well and has a distinct flavor, so skip it.

STORING SYRUPS

For the recipes in this book, I recommend storing your finished syrups in the refrigerator, which extends shelf life and retards the growth of any harmful bacteria. Just a few extra precautions will ensure that they'll keep as long and as safely as possible.

- Always remember to use clean storage containers; and when bottling soda syrups, make sure that the lids or tops are spotless as well as the glass or plastic bottles. The best way to sterilize is to put the containers and lids in a large pot, cover completely with water, and bring to a boil.

- Cover all bottles and jars tightly before refrigerating. If for any reason your food takes on an off color or smell over time, discard it. You can always make more!

RAW EGGS—SAFE OR NOT?

It's said that raw egg yolks taste of vanilla and that eating them enhances your health. But it's known that some raw eggs can carry the salmonella bacteria. In most cases, salmonella exists only on the shell, and some people feel comfortable simply washing the eggs or scalding them in boiling water for 5 seconds before cracking them open.

Since there is no way to guarantee that your eggs are 100 percent safe, you'll have to make the decision that's right for you. I recommend skipping them if you're in a high-risk group for infections, like pregnant women or people with compromised immune systems. I'll go ahead and say that I eat them regularly in egg shakes, holiday egg nog, on steak tartare, and in salad dressing. If you find a good source for fresh eggs and use smart kitchen hygiene, you should be fine.

SASSAFRAS

In the 1960s, there was a ban on food-grade sassafras plant components in the United States, based on some tests done on lab animals and a few case reports on people. Safrole, a chemical found in the plant, was linked to liver damage with extreme doses and heavy, long-term use. In 1994, the ban was reversed, allowing the sale of root extracts that don't contain safrole or from which the compound was removed.

SODA
SYRUPS
FROM THE
FARM

GRAPEFRUIT SYRUP

Tart and tangy, the flavor of grapefruit wakes the senses, and a soda made with this syrup is wonderful served as a bright, eye-opening breakfast treat. I like to balance the flavor with a little sugar and a small amount of salt to make a refreshing soda that tastes sunny and sophisticated. MAKES ABOUT 2½ CUPS

---

2 cups water

Pinch of salt

1½ cups sugar

Zest of 2 grapefruits

¾ cup fresh grapefruit juice

In a medium saucepan set over medium heat, bring the water, salt, and sugar to a boil. Add the zest and remove the pan from the heat. Cover the pan and steep for 20 minutes.

Add the juice to the pan and stir. Strain the syrup through a clean piece of cheesecloth and let cool. Store in an airtight container in the refrigerator for up to 7 days.

GRAPEFRUIT SODA

For one drink, fill a tall glass with ice. Add 3 tablespoons of the Grapefruit Syrup, top with seltzer, and mix gently.

SEVILLE ORANGE SYRUP

Also known as a sour orange or a bitter orange, the Seville orange is traditionally used in marmalade. The thick, deeply colored peel is valued for its fragrant oil, used widely in perfumes. When tempered with sweetness, the bold flavor of this exotic citrus fruit is amazing. Sodas made with this syrup are definitely not Fanta Orange. MAKES ABOUT 2 CUPS

1½ cups water

1 cup sugar

Zest of 4 Seville oranges

½ cup fresh orange juice (if not making a phosphate)

In a medium saucepan set over medium heat, bring the water and sugar to a boil. Turn off the heat, add the zest, cover the pan, and steep for 30 minutes.

Add the orange juice and stir, strain the syrup through a fine-mesh strainer, and let cool. Store in an airtight container in the refrigerator for up to 7 days.

SEVILLE ORANGE SODA

For one drink, fill a tall glass with ice. Add 3 tablespoons of the Seville Orange Syrup, top with seltzer, and mix gently.

STEP IT UP

- For a fizzy variation on the classic Screwdriver, add 1 ounce of vodka to the soda recipe.
- Make a version of this syrup to use in a classic orange phosphate by skipping the addition of the orange juice and adding a few drops of acid phosphate to the soda recipe.

LIME SYRUP

Citrus is the most common base for all sodas, so mastering a perfect lime or lemon syrup is a must for home soda makers. With a solid citrus soda in hand, branching out to mix syrups in the glass or even experimenting with extra flavors at the cooking stage is the next step. From that foundation, the creative possibilities grow exponentially. I find a Microplane zester, which completely avoids the bitter white pith, is absolutely indispensable for making a perfect citrus syrup. MAKES ABOUT 1½ CUPS

1¼ cups water

1 cup sugar

Zest of 4 limes

In a medium saucepan set over medium heat, bring the water and sugar to a boil. Add the zest and remove the pan from the heat. Steep for at least 1 hour.

Let cool. Store in an airtight container in the refrigerator for up to 14 days.

FRESH LIME SODA

For one drink, fill a tall glass with ice. Add 3 tablespoons of the Lime Syrup and the juice of half a lime. Top with seltzer and mix gently.

LEMON SYRUP

● Make a lemon syrup by substituting lemon zest for the lime.

CHERRY LIME RICKEY

MAKES 1 DRINK

Sweet and sour is the best way to describe this tangy-tart, brightly colored treat. Kids love it, and it's a great nonalcoholic offering for adult parties, too. It just feels more fun than drinking plain old fruit juice or seltzer with a wedge of lemon.

2 tablespoons Lime Syrup (page 23)

Juice of ½ lime

Dash of citric acid solution

Seltzer

2 tablespoons Sour Cherry Syrup (page 32)

Wedge of lime, for garnish

Fill a tall glass with ice. Add the lime syrup, lime juice, and citric acid solution. Add the seltzer, float the cherry syrup on top, and garnish with the lime wedge.

FOUNTAIN
FACT

The patent for the first marble soda fountain was granted in 1863, introducing an era when some conservatives called soda fountains "glorified halls of intoxication" because of their early associations with pharmaceuticals like cocaine, medicinal alcohol, and caffeine.

MEYER LEMON SYRUP

Smooth-skinned, plump, and almost neon yellow, Meyer lemons are low in acid, floral in fragrance, and almost sweet, like oranges. Their light, honey-like aroma makes these canary-colored treats a favorite of pastry chefs.

MAKES ABOUT 2 CUPS

1½ cups water

Pinch of salt

1 cup minus 1 tablespoon sugar

Zest of 4 Meyer lemons

In a medium saucepan set over medium heat, bring the water, salt, and sugar to a boil. Add the zest and remove the pan from the heat. Cover the pan and steep for 20 minutes.

Strain the syrup through a fine-mesh strainer and let cool. Store in an airtight container in the refrigerator for up to 7 days.

MEYER LEMON SODA

For one drink, fill a tall glass with ice. Add 3 tablespoons of the Meyer Lemon Syrup from Zest, the juice from half a Meyer lemon, and top with seltzer.

MEYER LEMON LACTART

For one drink, fill a tall glass with ice. Add 3 tablespoons of the Meyer Lemon Syrup from Zest and 1 teaspoon lactic acid. Top with seltzer and mix gently.

GINGER SYRUP

A basic, must-have ingredient for the serious soda crafter, ginger syrup is an excellent starter recipe. Stirred into a glass of icy seltzer, it makes a zingy, invigorating soda with just enough bite to be interesting. As a building block for more complicated drink blends, this syrup adds depth with its warm spice and clean citrus note. For a more traditional ginger syrup that will make a classic ginger ale, omit the lemon zest. MAKES ABOUT 1½ CUPS

2 ounces fresh unpeeled ginger (about the size of the first part of your thumb)

1 cup water

¾ cup sugar

2 pieces lemon zest

Wash the ginger well in hot water. Using a Microplane zester, grate the ginger, carefully reserving the juice and pulp.

In a medium saucepan set over medium heat, bring the water and sugar to a gentle boil. Add the ginger and lemon zest, and remove the pan from the heat. Cover the pan and steep for about 45 minutes.

Strain the syrup through a fine-mesh strainer and let cool. Store in an airtight container in the refrigerator for up to 14 days.

GINGER ALE

For one drink, fill a tall glass with ice. Add 3 tablespoons of the Ginger Syrup, 1 tablespoon of fresh lemon juice, top with seltzer, and mix gently.

GUAVA SYRUP

Guava is a small fruit with big flavor. Its fragrance is reminiscent of a lemon rind, but more floral and less sharp. With a pulp that tastes like the offspring of a pear and a strawberry, its popularity in tropical locales around the globe is no surprise. **MAKES ABOUT 2½ CUPS**

2 pounds fresh guava

2 cups water

1 cup minus 1 tablespoon sugar

Cut the guava into ½-inch slices, and put them into a heatproof bowl.

Bring the water and sugar to a boil in a medium saucepan and carefully pour it over the guava slices. Using a potato masher, mash the guava thoroughly. Cover and let cool to room temperature. Refrigerate the guava overnight.

The following day, strain the syrup through a fine-mesh strainer and discard the fruit solids. Store the syrup in an airtight container in the refrigerator for up to 7 days.

GUAVA SODA

For one drink, fill a tall glass with ice. Add 3 tablespoons of the Guava Syrup, 1 tablespoon of fresh lemon juice, top with seltzer, and mix gently.

PINEAPPLE SYRUP

The concentrated sweet, slightly tangy flavor of this pineapple syrup is a universal favorite. Ripe pineapples organically balance the sweetness and tartness, so they're a natural for cool, fresh sodas. The lemon juice tones down the sugar, making this treat a grown-up favorite. **MAKES ABOUT 2 CUPS**

---

2 cups fresh pineapple juice

1 tablespoon fresh lemon juice

1 tablespoon water

¾ cup sugar

In a medium saucepan set over medium heat, bring the pineapple juice, lemon juice, water, and sugar to a simmer, but not a rolling boil. Simmer until the sugar is dissolved, about 2 minutes. Remove the pan from the heat and let cool. Store in an airtight container in the refrigerator for up to 5 days.

PINEAPPLE SODA

For one drink, fill a tall glass with ice. Add 3 tablespoons of the Pineapple Syrup, top with seltzer, and mix gently.

STEP IT UP

- Add a shot of Myers's Dark Rum to the basic soda recipe for a tropical cocktail.

ROCKAWAY BEACH CLUB

MAKES 1 DRINK

Sometimes a cocktail is called for, and sometimes, so is a clear head. Whether you're serving colleagues at an out-of-office retreat or parents who have to drive the school-run after a brunch, this island-inspired soda is a refreshing change from plain punches and standard commercial sodas.

FOUNTAIN FACT

Dating back to ancient times, natural spring mineral water was thought to have curative and restorative powers, just short of miraculous. Drunk straight, or flavored with herbs or honey, the fizzy beverage was both a tasty treat and a medicine for the masses.

2 tablespoons Pineapple Syrup (page 29)

Seltzer

1½ teaspoons Lime Syrup (page 23)

1 tablespoon Hibiscus Syrup (page 70)

Pineapple wedge, for garnish

Lime wheel, for garnish

Fill a tall glass with ice. Add the pineapple syrup, then pour in the seltzer until the glass is almost full. Top with the lime syrup, then the hibiscus syrup. Garnish with a pineapple wedge and a lime wheel. If you have a few paper umbrellas, so much the better!

SOUR CHERRY SYRUP

Since the fruit is tart and acidic, the taste for sour cherries right off the tree is an acquired one. When tamed with sweeteners, like sugar or honey, this fruit becomes a natural for liqueurs, preserves, and syrups. **MAKES ABOUT 2 CUPS**

2 quarts fresh sour cherries, pitted

2 cups sugar

Juice of ½ lemon

In a medium saucepan set over medium heat, combine the cherries, sugar, and lemon juice and bring to a boil. Simmer for 30 minutes.

Strain the syrup through a fine-mesh strainer and discard the fruit solids. Store the syrup in an airtight container in the refrigerator for up to 7 days.

STEP IT UP

- For a deeper, more lush cherry flavor with more sweetness than bite, substitute sweet dark cherries for the sour cherries, or try a mix of the two to suit your own taste preference.

- Pour this syrup over a scoop of chocolate ice cream to mimic the flavor of chocolate-covered cherry cordials. Or stir it into milk for a Valentine's Day breakfast treat.

POMEGRANATE SYRUP (AKA GRENADINE)

Why buy bottles of grenadine when it's so easy to make at home, the natural way? This garnet-hued, sweetly piquant syrup is a great addition to any number of beverages for both its color and its flavor—and it makes a delicious soda on its own, too. Use high-quality bottled pomegranate juice, or make your own using the tips on page 34. MAKES ABOUT 2½ CUPS

2 cups pomegranate juice

1 cup caster sugar

Pinch of salt

Combine the pomegranate juice, sugar, and salt in a tightly lidded container. Shake until the sugar is dissolved. Store in an airtight container for up to 14 days.

JUICING
POMEGRANATES

Pomegranates are a little tricky, but fresh juice is hard to beat. Start by separating the seeds from the skin and pith: Cut the fruit in half crosswise. Hold one half upside down over a large bowl, and using a heavy spoon, strike the back of the peel repeatedly. The seeds will pop out into the bowl. There are a few ways to juice this fruit:

- Put the seeds in a zip-top bag and gently crush with a rolling pin. Be careful not to bear down too hard, as chemicals from the seeds could impart a bitter taste to the juice. Strain the mixture through a clean piece of cheesecloth or a coffee filter, then discard the pulp.

- Pulse the seeds in a conventional blender, then strain as above.

- Run the seeds through a food mill, discarding the pulp.

- Instead of extracting the seeds, ream halves of the fruit on a citrus juicer, as you would a lemon.

HOW TO ZEST
CITRUS

Mastering the skill of zesting citrus is key to making the finest soda syrups.

1 Wash the fruit thoroughly.

2 Cradle the fruit in your palm from end to end, so that one tip is near your pinkie and one tip is near your thumb, in order to expose the most zest.

3 Prop the zester against a flat cutting board, holding it at a 45-degree angle.

4 With one broad stroke, scrape the fruit against the zester from tip to tail while twisting your wrist. Grate shallowly to avoid the bitter white pith. With a larger fruit, you may not be able to zest the full strip at one time.

5 Spin the fruit on an orbit, repeating the zesting motion, until the whole fruit is scraped clean of zest.

ANTON'S SHIRLEY TEMPLE

MAKES 1 DRINK

Legend has it that a bartender at Chasen's, the famous West Hollywood gathering place for entertainment luminaries, created the eponymous cocktail for "Little Curly Top," the star of *Bright Eyes, Little Miss Marker,* and *The Littlest Rebel.* Necessarily nonalcoholic, the drink's appeal to children may lie in the brightly colored, candy-sweet maraschino cherry garnish.

FOUNTAIN FACT

Responding to the new negative reputation of soda fountains as places that sell intoxicating beverages, the Harrison Act was passed in 1914, which limited the sale of cocaine and other opiates without a prescription.

2 tablespoons Ginger Syrup (page 27)

½ cup fresh orange juice

Seltzer

Dash of Pomegranate Syrup (page 33)

Maraschino cherry, for garnish

Fill a tall glass with ice. Add the ginger syrup and orange juice, and pour in enough seltzer to fill the glass. Add a dash of the pomegranate syrup, garnish with the cherry, and serve.

BLUEBERRY SYRUP

If you're lucky enough to forage for your own berries, this recipe is an excellent way to make the most of your haul. But a summer trip to the farmer's market or produce department will yield plenty of fresh pints for that bursting sweet taste that encapsulates the feeling of hot-weather picnics and the Fourth of July. MAKES ABOUT 2 CUPS

1½ cups fresh blueberries

1 cup sugar

1 tablespoon fresh lemon juice

In a small saucepan set over medium heat, combine the blueberries, sugar, and lemon juice. Bring to a simmer slowly, stirring until all of the berries have popped, about 10 minutes. Remove the pan from the heat and let cool. Transfer the mixture to an airtight container and refrigerate overnight.

The next day, remove the mixture from the refrigerator. Strain the syrup through a fine-mesh strainer. Store in an airtight container in the refrigerator for up to 5 days.

BLUEBERRY SODA

For one drink, fill a tall glass with ice. Add 3 tablespoons of the Blueberry Syrup, top with seltzer, and mix gently.

BASIL SYRUP

With its mild, peppery flavor and delicate menthol aroma, basil features prominently in Italian, Thai, and Vietnamese cuisine. Varieties include sweet basil, lemon basil, chocolate basil, pineapple basil, and the slightly astringent holy basil. Experiment to find out which one is your favorite for this herbal-sweet syrup. MAKES ABOUT 3 CUPS

2 cups water

1⅔ cups sugar

25 large fresh basil leaves

In a medium saucepan set over medium heat, bring the water and sugar to a boil. Add the basil leaves and cover the pan. Steep for 15 minutes.

Strain the syrup through a fine-mesh strainer, discard the leaves, and let cool. Store the syrup in an airtight container in the refrigerator for up to 4 days.

BASIL SODA

For one drink, fill a tall glass with ice. Add 3 tablespoons of the Basil Syrup, top with seltzer, and mix gently.

MINT SYRUP

• Make a fresh mint syrup by substituting mint leaves for basil leaves.

STEP IT UP

• Try drizzling the syrup over cubes of fresh cantaloupe for a refreshing snack or dessert.

ANISE HYSSOP SYRUP

Also known as licorice mint, the anise hyssop plant is technically neither. With its many culinary uses, it's a great addition to a home garden, but beware: it reseeds itself and can take over very quickly. You can generally find it at farmer's markets and upscale produce stores that carry a wide variety of herbs.

Sweet, rather than spicy to the taste, anise hyssop is a natural for desserts and soft drinks. I like using these flowers over fruit salad, for their unique taste that's faintly reminiscent of licorice and lavender, and for their beauty. The plant's leaves can be dried and used in tea, for a clean, palate-cleansing drink. Anise hyssop makes a sophisticated soda, great to serve at celebrations in place of cocktails or wine. MAKES ABOUT 3 CUPS

---

2 cups water

1½ cups sugar

1 bunch fresh anise hyssop (reserve some of the flowers for garnish)

In a medium saucepan set over medium heat, bring the water and sugar to a boil. Add the anise hyssop and cover the pan. Steep for 15 minutes.

Strain the syrup through a fine-mesh strainer, discard the solids, and let cool. Store the syrup in an airtight container in the refrigerator for up to 4 days.

STEP IT UP

● An acid note is also a nice touch with the exotic herbal flavor of this drink. Try adding a few drops of lactic acid or lemon juice to the basic soda recipe.

ANISE HYSSOP SODA

For one drink, fill a tall glass with ice. Add 3 tablespoons of the Anise Hyssop Syrup, top with seltzer, and mix gently. Garnish with the reserved anise hyssop flowers.

LEMON VERBENA SYRUP

Some describe the flavor of lemon verbena as a cross between a very subtle licorice and camphor. I love it for its lemony finish. Herbal and bright, it's sometimes used in cooking as a replacement for oregano. As a soda flavor, lemon verbena is modern and crisp, with an herbal complexity. It's great as a stand-alone drink for cocktail hour and as a complement to light, simple meals. MAKES ABOUT 3 CUPS

2 cups water

1 2/3 cups sugar

20 to 30 large fresh lemon verbena leaves

In a medium saucepan set over medium heat, bring the water and sugar to a boil. Add the lemon verbena leaves and cover the pan. Steep for 15 minutes.

Strain the syrup through a fine-mesh strainer, discard the leaves, and let cool. Store the syrup in an airtight container in the refrigerator for up to 4 days.

CHERRY VERBENA SODA

For one drink, fill a tall glass with ice. Add 1 tablespoon of the Lemon Verbena Syrup, 2 tablespoons of Sour Cherry Syrup (page 32), and a few dashes of acid phosphate or lemon juice or citric acid solution. Top with seltzer and mix gently. Garnish with lemon verbena leaves and maraschino cherries, if desired.

TELL ME ABOUT
LEMON
VERBENA

Sometimes called "The Queen of the Lemon-Scented Herbs," lemon verbena was a favorite ingredient in perfumes in late 1700s Europe, and it had a moment of fame in *Gone with the Wind,* as it was Scarlett's mother's favorite plant. The leaves of lemon verbena are great in cooking, as they impart a lemony fragrance and flavor to dishes ranging from broiled fish, to salad dressings, to light desserts. As a beverage, it is used to make herbal tea and is often added to black tea in place of lemon.

LEMONGRASS SYRUP

Commonly used in soups, teas, and curries, lemongrass both dried and fresh imparts a bright citrus flavor to dishes. The oil of the lemongrass plant acts as a preservative and is used widely in aromatherapy, owing to its heady perfume. MAKES ABOUT 2½ CUPS

3 stalks lemongrass

2 cups water

1½ cups sugar

1 thick strip of lemon zest

Wash the lemongrass, smash it with the butt end of a knife, then thinly slice it.

In a medium saucepan set over medium heat, bring the water and sugar to a boil. Add the lemongrass and lemon zest, and remove the pan from the heat. Steep for 1 hour.

Strain the syrup through a fine-mesh strainer, discard the solids, and let cool. Store the syrup in an airtight container in the refrigerator for up to 14 days.

GINGER LEMONGRASS SODA

For one drink, fill a tall glass with ice. Add 1 tablespoon of the Lemongrass Syrup, 1 tablespoon of Ginger Syrup (page 27), and the juice of half a lemon or lime, or a few drops of citric acid solution. Top with seltzer and mix gently.

CONCORD GRAPE SYRUP

Rich, jewel-colored, and fragrant, this syrup wows wine lovers and grape soda lovers alike. The highly aromatic Concord grape is a natural for juicing, with a flavor leaning toward candied strawberries and musk. Even when mixed with seltzer, this syrup never tastes watered down. MAKES ABOUT 3 CUPS

---

2 quarts fresh Concord grapes

2 cups sugar

Juice of ½ lemon

In a medium saucepan set over medium heat, combine the grapes, sugar, and lemon juice and bring to a simmer. Cook for 30 minutes.

Strain the syrup through a fine-mesh strainer, discard the solids, and let cool. Store the syrup in an airtight container in the refrigerator for up to 5 days.

GRAPE PHOSPHATE

For one drink, fill a tall glass with ice. Add 3 tablespoons of the Concord Grape Syrup and a few dashes of acid phosphate. Top with seltzer and mix gently.

THE CONCORD GRAPE, AN AMERICAN ORIGINAL

Hailing from the town of Concord, Massachusetts, the first Concord grape was cultivated in the mid-1800s. Unlike many of its European ancestors, this robust grape thrives in the rugged New England soil and ripens early, allowing it to escape the early fall frosts. Prized for their pungent aroma and deep, jammy flavor, the dark purple-skinned grapes are the most popular variety sold in the United States.

HUCKLEBERRY SYRUP

Huckleberries are not commercially cultivated, so devotees will have to find them in the wild or purchase them from a forager. Often confused with blueberries, these purple-black beauties are decidedly tarter and have a more complex flavor than their cousins. "Imagine eating wildness," rhapsodizes 'Asta Bowen in her 1998 handbook *The Huckleberry Book*. For a soda that tastes of all the freshness nature has to offer, you can't go wrong choosing the huckleberry as a base. **MAKES ABOUT 3 CUPS**

---

2 cups fresh huckleberries

1¼ cups sugar

1 cup water

1 teaspoon fresh lemon juice

Pinch of salt

In a small saucepan set over medium heat, combine the berries, sugar, water, lemon juice, and salt. Slowly bring the mixture to a simmer, stirring until all of the berries have popped, about 5 minutes (you can also mash with a potato masher). Remove the pan from the heat and let cool. Transfer the mixture to an airtight container and refrigerate overnight.

The next day, strain the syrup through a fine-mesh strainer and discard the solids. Store the syrup in an airtight container in the refrigerator for up to 5 days.

HUCKLEBERRY SODA

For one drink, fill a tall glass with ice. Add 3 tablespoons of the Huckleberry Syrup, top with seltzer, and mix gently.

ELDERBERRY SYRUP

- In sharp contrast to the complicated, full-bodied taste of the huckleberry is the lighter, more subtle taste of elderberry. The elderberry's delicate flavor is floral and fruity at the same time, reminiscent of the lychee's. The components of the elderberry tree (*Sambucus nigras*) are used to flavor elderflower cordial, the Italian liqueur Sambuca, and the French liqueur St-Germain. It even plays a key role in Fanta's Shokata soft drink. The berries are used in pies, marmalade, relishes, and now, soda.

- To make elderberry syrup, prepare the Huckleberry Syrup recipe, substituting elderberries for huckleberries. For one drink, fill a tall glass with ice. Add 3 tablespoons of the elderberry syrup, top with seltzer, and mix gently.

FOUNTAIN FACT

From the early 1800s to the 1960s, soda fountains and ice cream parlors were often housed under pharmacies' roofs, providing one-stop shopping for medicines and refreshments. The dispenser or pharmacist, who had the chemical knowledge to mix healing potions, evolved into the bartender of the Prohibition era. Don't let the name fool you: these soda jerks were considered cool, and their jobs were highly coveted.

CRANBERRY SPICE SYRUP

This is a special flavor I perfected for my friends Harry and Taylor at The Brooklyn Kitchen, where I teach my soda-making class. The mixture of fresh and dried berries balances the flavor notes of this syrup: the fresh berries lend a sun-kissed brightness while the dried berries ground it with deep, dark tones—rich and perfect for the winter holiday season.

MAKES ABOUT 3 CUPS

---

1 cup fresh cranberries (about 3 ounces)

¾ cup dried cranberries (about 2 ounces)

2 cups water

1 cup sugar

2 pieces orange zest

2 coin-size slices of fresh ginger

6 allspice berries

1 cinnamon stick

2 whole cloves

Pinch of salt

In a medium saucepan set over low heat, combine the fresh and dried cranberries, water, sugar, zest, ginger, allspice, cinnamon stick, cloves, and salt. Cook until the cranberries burst, about 15 minutes. Remove the pan from the heat and let cool.

Strain the syrup through a fine-mesh strainer and discard the solids. Store the syrup in an airtight container in the refrigerator for up to 7 days.

CRANBERRY SPICE SODA

For one drink, fill a tall glass with ice. Add 3 tablespoons of the Cranberry Spice Syrup, top with seltzer, and mix gently.

QUINCE SYRUP

A unique fruit, the quince has a floral fragrance and pear-like shape. A sacred symbol of Aphrodite, the quince was used as a breath-freshener by brides in ancient Greece, who would nibble on the fruit to perfume their kisses.

Don't waste the cooked fruit pulp after you've strained out the syrup! Puree it in a food processor until it's soft like jam and use it as a spread to pair with Manchego cheese, a Spanish variety made with sheep's milk, or salty Greek Mizithra cheese, which is a lot like feta, but firmer. For more texture, serve alongside almonds or walnuts. **MAKES ABOUT 3 CUPS**

---

4 large quinces

6 cups water

2½ cups sugar

Juice of 1 lemon

1 (2-inch-long) strip of lemon zest

1 teaspoon salt

Wash the quinces thoroughly with warm water, rubbing them to remove the fuzz. Peel the quinces, cut in half, and remove the core and seeds. Dice the fruit into large pieces, and put in a medium saucepan with the water, sugar, lemon juice and zest, and salt. Set the pan over medium heat and bring the mixture to a simmer. Cover and cook for 3 hours, or until the liquid is a dark auburn color. Strain the syrup through a fine-mesh strainer, reserving the fruit for another use. Store in an airtight container in the refrigerator for up to 7 days.

QUINCE SODA

For one drink, fill a tall glass with ice. Add 3 tablespoons of the Quince Syrup, top with seltzer, and mix gently.

BANANA SYRUP

Sweet, spicy, and full-bodied, this syrup reminds me of stacks of pancakes, French toast dusted with sugar, and pudding. The coconut sugar lends a nice touch of tropical essence, as well as a depth of flavor that you can't get from any other sugar. You can find coconut sugar in the natural-foods section of most large grocery stores. **MAKES ABOUT 1 CUP**

1½ cups caster sugar

2 tablespoons maple sugar (see Sources, page 141)

2 tablespoons coconut sugar

4 large bananas, peeled

Juice of ½ lemon

In a medium bowl, combine the sugars. Slice the bananas into ¼-inch rounds, then toss the pieces in the sugar mixture, coating them thoroughly. Add the lemon juice, toss well, and transfer to an airtight container. Store the mixture in the refrigerator for 2 days.

After 2 days, strain the mixture through a colander, pressing on the banana solids to extract the liquid. Discard the banana solids. Store the syrup in an airtight container in the refrigerator for up to 5 days.

BANANA SODA

For one drink, fill a tall glass with ice. Add 3 tablespoons of the Banana Syrup, top with seltzer, and mix gently.

EIGHT-HOUR MEYER
LEMONS IN SYRUP

Urbane, clean, and with a mild bitter finish, this syrup makes a one-of-a-kind base for a soda or a cocktail. I really enjoy the balance of sweet and bitter flavors that develops from slowly cooking a blend of peel and whole fruit. MAKES ONE 16-OUNCE JAR

6 Meyer lemons

1½ cups sugar

¼ teaspoon salt

Bring a large pot of water to a boil. Meanwhile, wash the lemons and slice them into ⅛-inch-thick rounds. Remove the seeds.

Combine the sugar and salt in a large bowl, add the lemon slices, and toss well. Arrange the lemon slices in layers in a sterilized, wide-mouthed 16-ounce canning jar, sprinkling any extra salt and sugar mixture between the layers. Cover the jar with its lid, put it in the pot of boiling water, and reduce the heat until the water is simmering. Simmer in the water bath at about 200°F (use a candy thermometer) for 8 hours. If need be, add a little water to the pot as it boils off.

Carefully remove the jar from the pot and let cool completely on the counter. The lemons will keep in the refrigerator, unopened, for several months. Once the jar has been opened, the lemons will keep for up to 14 days.

BITTER LEMON SODA

This lemon soda has a dry, slightly bitter taste that reminds me of European soft drinks like Chinotto, Sanbitter, and Bitter Kas. Modern and cosmopolitan, it's definitely not your grandmother's lemonade!

For one drink, fill a tall glass with ice. Add 3 tablespoons of the syrup from the cooked lemons, top with seltzer, and mix gently.

CANDIED KUMQUATS IN SYRUP

Available in two varieties, round and oval, the kumquat is considered a symbol of good luck in many Asian cultures and is often given as a gift during the Lunar New Year. Popular as a houseplant, its branches are inclined to be groomed for bonsai.

In cultures where the kumquat is popular, the raw fruit is sometimes eaten whole, the contrast of the sweet peel and the tart fruit being a prized, albeit acquired, taste.

Because of their delicate hue, kumquats have become popular in the West, sliced in green salads and as a cocktail garnish. When the kumquat is preserved with sugar in relishes, marmalades, beverage syrups, and as candied fruit, its tart nature is toned and tamed, and the floral fragrance shines as a winning trait. **MAKES ONE 8-OUNCE JAR**

¾ cup kumquats

Pinch of salt

⅓ cup sugar

⅓ cup water

Bring a large pot of water to a boil. Meanwhile, put the kumquats in a medium saucepan, cover with water, and add the salt. Set the pan over high heat and bring to a boil. Remove the pan from the heat and strain the mixture through a colander, discarding the water. Put the kumquats back into the saucepan and cover with water. Bring the kumquats back to a boil and repeat the process, blanching the fruit a total of three times to help remove some of the bitterness.

After the final blanching, put the fruit in a sterilized, wide-mouthed 8-ounce canning jar, and add the sugar and ⅓ cup water. Cover the jar with its lid, put it in the pot of boiling water, and reduce the heat until the water is simmering. Simmer in the water bath at 190°F (use a candy thermometer) for 2 hours, or until the kumquats start to look translucent. Avoid a rolling boil, or the kumquats will burst. Add a little water to the pot as it boils off.

Carefully remove the jar from the pot and let cool completely on the counter. The kumquats will keep in the refrigerator, unopened, for several months. Once the jar has been opened, the kumquats will keep for up to 14 days.

KUMQUAT SODA

The syrup from the Candied Kumquats has an amazing tart, sour-orange flavor with just enough sweetness. For one drink, fill a tall glass with ice. Add 3 tablespoons of the syrup, top with seltzer, and mix gently. Garnish with some slices of the Candied Kumquats.

FOUNTAIN
FACT

Soda fountains hit their heyday in the early 1900s, with the invention and accessibility of carbon dioxide tanks. Historical recipes often include mentions of "ounces of sherry" or "dashes of liqueur, such as crème de menthe," proving that soda fountains weren't just child's play.

SODA
SYRUPS
FROM THE
PANTRY

CHOCOLATE SYRUP

Reminiscent of your favorite sundae sauce, but better! A sip of soda made from this deep, dark, intense brew is like chomping down on a chocolate bar.

MAKES ABOUT 3 CUPS

---

2 cups water

1 cup plus 2 tablespoons sugar

Pinch of salt

¼ vanilla bean, halved

2 tablespoons chocolate husks (optional; see page 134)

3 tablespoons Scharffen Berger or other high-quality cocoa powder

In a medium saucepan set over medium heat, bring the water, sugar, and salt to a boil. Remove the pan from the heat. Scrape the seeds of the vanilla bean into the pan, toss in the pod, and add the chocolate husks (if using). Steep for 10 minutes.

Put the cocoa powder in a large bowl. Strain the steeped liquid through a fine-mesh strainer into the cocoa and whisk until smooth. Return the mixture to the saucepan and bring to a boil over medium heat. Reduce to a simmer and cook for 2 minutes, stirring constantly. Strain the mixture again, and then let cool. Store in an airtight container in the refrigerator for up to 14 days.

CHOCOLATE PHOSPHATE

For one drink, fill a glass with ice. Add 3 tablespoons of the Chocolate Syrup and half a teaspoon of acid phosphate, top with seltzer, and mix gently.

VANILLA SYRUP

Like Torani, but better, because this syrup is all-natural and comes out of your own kitchen. Put the money you'll save from not buying Starbucks into a jar and indulge in this inexpensive treat. MAKES ABOUT 3 CUPS

2 cups water

2 cups sugar

3 vanilla beans, halved

In a medium saucepan set over medium heat, bring the water and sugar to a boil. Scrape the seeds of the vanilla beans into the pan and toss in the pods. Remove the pan from the heat and let cool to room temperature. Store the syrup in the refrigerator in an airtight container for up to 14 days. Do not strain at this stage—leaving the pods in the syrup deepens the flavor. Strain before using.

BLUEBERRY-VANILLA PHOSPHATE

For one drink, fill a glass with ice. Add 2 tablespoons of Blueberry Syrup (page 36), 1 tablespoon of the Vanilla Syrup, and half a teaspoon of acid phosphate. Top with seltzer and mix gently.

SARSAPARILLA SYRUP

Sarsaparilla, along with sassafras, is one of the main flavors in old-fashioned root beer. Popular in the American West during the pioneer period, sarsaparilla-based drinks have become more of a novelty drink in the United States. In Louisiana Cajun country, people dry and grind the leaves of the sassafras tree to make filé powder, an ingredient in gumbo. MAKES ABOUT 2½ CUPS

2 cups water

1¾ cups sugar

4 ounces dried sarsaparilla root

1 ounce dried birch root

Pinch of salt

In a medium saucepan over high heat, bring the water and sugar to a boil. Remove the pan from the heat and add the sarsaparilla root, birch root, and salt. Steep for exactly 35 minutes. (If it steeps any longer, it will taste too woodsy, but steeped any less and it will be thin.) Strain immediately through a fine-mesh strainer, discard the roots, and let cool. Store the syrup in an airtight container in the refrigerator for up to 7 days.

SARSAPARILLA SODA

For one drink, fill a tall glass with ice. Add 3 tablespoons of the Sarsaparilla Syrup, top with seltzer, and mix gently.

TOASTED ALMOND SYRUP

I love this syrup with hot drinks, and its slightly bitter, nutty flavor is a natural to pair with biscotti, fruit pastry, and hot cocoa. MAKES ABOUT ¾ CUP

1 cup blanched almonds

1 cup sugar

1½ cups boiling water

Preheat the oven to 350°F.

Spread the almonds out on a baking sheet. Put the pan in the oven and toast the almonds, stirring occasionally with a wooden spoon, until golden brown, about 5 minutes. Let cool slightly.

Combine the toasted almonds and the sugar in the bowl of a food processor and pulse until ground, but avoid making the nuts powdery. Put the mixture in a heatproof bowl and pour in the boiling water. Stir until the sugar is completely dissolved, then let cool. Cover the bowl and chill in the refrigerator overnight.

Strain the syrup through a clean piece of cheesecloth or a coffee filter. Store the syrup in an airtight container in the refrigerator for up to 7 days.

(RECIPE CONTINUES)

TOASTED ALMOND SODA

For one drink, fill a tall glass with ice. Add 3 tablespoons of the Toasted Almond Syrup, top with
seltzer, and stir well.

CHOCOLATE-ALMOND SODA

Like a liquid Hershey's with Almonds, this soda is
the perfect remedy when you're thirsty and crave
a sweet goody. For one drink, fill a tall glass with
ice. Add 1 tablespoon of the Toasted Almond Syrup
and 2 tablespoons of Chocolate Syrup (page 56),
top with seltzer, and mix gently.

COFFEE SYRUP

At the intersection of gourmet soda and coffee culture lies Manhattan Soda Company's Pure Espresso Coffee Soda, a thirst-quencher and pick-me-up that's been popular since 1895. Cold brewed, with added chicory for smoothness, my coffee syrup is a nod to the venerable favorite. Make sure to use a dark roast, like French roast, for the fullest flavor. You can buy chicory from Louisiana's Community Coffee Company (see Sources, page 141), known for blending it with their ground coffee beans for a traditional Cajun-style brew, and it can easily be found at bulk-food stores, at health-food stores, from Internet wholesalers, and now in many major supermarkets. MAKES ABOUT 1 CUP

1¼ cups water

1 cup medium-grind coffee

¾ cup caster sugar

¼ cup chicory root

STEP IT UP

- Add 2 tablespoons of the Coffee Syrup to a vanilla milkshake for a frozen mocha.

In a very large bowl, combine the water, coffee, sugar, and chicory. Stir until well combined and transfer to the refrigerator. Steep for 24 hours.

Put a fine-mesh strainer over a large bowl and line it with cheesecloth or coffee filters. Slowly pour the liquid through the strainer. This is a slow process and will need to be done in small batches. Push the last of the liquid through with the back of a spoon. Pour the syrup into an airtight container and shake until the sugar is completely dissolved. Store in the refrigerator for up to 5 days.

COFFEE SODA

For one drink, fill a tall glass with ice. Add 3 tablespoons of the Coffee Syrup, top with seltzer, and mix gently.

CREAM SODA SYRUP

Rich, full-bodied, and bursting with vanilla and caramel flavors, this syrup—along with lime, ginger, and hibiscus—is one of my most popular. In fact, it's Martha Stewart's favorite, too, as she told me when I first appeared on her show! MAKES ABOUT 3 CUPS

2 cups water

Juice of 1 lemon

2 cups sugar

2 vanilla beans, split and scraped

Pinch of salt

STEP IT UP

- **For perfect caramel, keep a close eye on the pot, as sugar burns easily.**

- **The vanilla beans can be removed the next day or left in to extract more flavor.**

In a small bowl, combine the water and lemon juice. Put the sugar in a heavy-bottomed pot with high sides, adding enough of the lemon water to make it look like wet sand, about $\frac{1}{4}$ cup. Cover the pot and bring the sugar to a boil. Reduce the heat to medium and cook, without stirring, until the sugar turns a dark amber color; look for a temperature of 280°F to 300°F on a candy thermometer. Remove the pot from the heat and let cool for 5 minutes.

Slowly and carefully, pour in the rest of the lemon water. Add the vanilla beans and salt, stir well, and bring the mixture to a simmer. Remove the pan from the heat and let cool to room temperature. Transfer to an airtight container and store in the refrigerator with the vanilla beans still in the liquid. Store the syrup in the refrigerator for up to 7 days.

CREAM SODA

For one drink, fill a tall glass with ice. Add a few dashes of lactic acid and 3 tablespoons of the Cream Soda Syrup. Top with seltzer and mix gently.

BOILED APPLE SYRUP

This recipe is basically a technique for a reduction, which produces a concentrated flavor that's never watered down. The syrup is very appley, perfect on its own, but also great if you add spices like nutmeg and clove. **MAKES ABOUT 2 CUPS**

½ gallon fresh apple juice

Pinch of salt

In a medium saucepan set over medium heat, bring the juice and salt to a simmer, but not a boil. Cook slowly until the juice is reduced by half, about 1 hour. Remove the pan from the heat and let cool. Store the syrup in an airtight container in the refrigerator for up to 7 days.

APPLE SODA

For one drink, fill a tall glass with ice. Add 3 tablespoons of the Boiled Apple Syrup. Top with seltzer and mix gently.

STEP IT UP
- Stir in 2 tablespoons of dark rum and 1 tablespoon of maple syrup for an autumn cocktail.

DRIED APRICOT AND BURDOCK SYRUP

The root of the burdock plant has been used in brewing beverages since medieval times, enjoying a starring role in hedgerow mead, an early relative of beer. It's chosen as an ingredient for its bitter flavor, which helps achieve balance in this soda syrup, the way that hops are used in modern-day beer to add an earthy element to the taste. MAKES ABOUT 1½ CUPS

1½ cups water

1 cup sugar

5 ounces dried apricots, cut into quarters

1 teaspoon dried burdock root, in a tea bag or tied into a piece of cheesecloth

Pinch of salt

In a medium saucepan set over medium heat, bring the water and sugar to a boil. Put the dried apricots, burdock, and salt into a large heatproof bowl. Pour the hot liquid over the fruit and root, and steep for 20 minutes. Remove the burdock, let the mixture cool, store in a lidded container, and refrigerate overnight.

The next day, strain the syrup through a fine-mesh strainer, using a large spoon to force as much liquid as possible from the apricots; discard the apricots. Store the syrup in an airtight container in the refrigerator for up to 7 days.

DRIED APRICOT AND BURDOCK SODA

For one drink, fill a tall glass with ice. Add 3 table-spoons of the Dried Apricot and Burdock Syrup, top with seltzer, and mix gently.

LAVENDER
GOLDEN RAISIN SYRUP

Fragrant, but never perfumey, the floral aroma and honeyed sweetness of this syrup bring to mind picnics in Provence. The fruitiness of the golden raisins ensures that the lavender isn't overwhelming, instead allowing it to provide a soft finish. **MAKES 3 CUPS**

---

2 cups water

1½ cups sugar

2 tablespoons golden raisins

¼ teaspoon dried lavender

Pinch of salt

In a medium saucepan set over medium heat, bring the water and sugar to a boil. Remove the pan from the heat and add the raisins, lavender, and salt. Steep for 1 hour.

Strain the syrup through a fine-mesh strainer, pushing firmly on the raisins with the back of a large spoon to remove as much liquid as possible; discard the raisins. Store the syrup in an airtight container in the refrigerator for up to 7 days.

LAVENDER GOLDEN RAISIN SODA

For one drink, fill a tall glass with ice. Add 3 tablespoons of the Lavender Golden Raisin Syrup, top with seltzer, and mix gently. If you like, garnish with food-grade lavender.

SPICED MAPLE SYRUP

The warming spices of winter conjure up thoughts of mulled wine and spiced cider drunk in the crisp breezes of the season. Add a dash to hard cider for a convivial evening warmer. This winning basic syrup can be blended with spirits for toddies or added to coffees and to drinking chocolate.

MAKES ABOUT 1 CUP

---

1 cinnamon stick

6 allspice berries

2 whole cloves

1 cardamom pod

**1 cup maple syrup
(dark amber Grade B
is best)**

In a medium heavy-bottomed saucepan set over high heat, combine the cinnamon stick, allspice, cloves, and cardamom. Toast the spices, pushing them around with a wooden spoon so that they don't burn, for 3 minutes or until they become fragrant. Add the maple syrup and bring the mixture to a light simmer. Remove the pan from the heat and let cool. Chill the syrup overnight in an airtight container in the refrigerator.

The next day, strain the syrup through a fine-mesh strainer and discard the spices. Store in an airtight container in the refrigerator for up to 14 days.

MAPLE-APPLE SPARKLER

For one drink, fill a tall glass with ice. Add 2 tablespoons of Boiled Apple Syrup (page 64), 1 tablespoon of the Spiced Maple Syrup, and a dash of acid phosphate. Top with seltzer, mix gently, and garnish with a cinnamon stick.

CHAMOMILE SYRUP

Made from the chamomile plant, purported to have calming qualities, this versatile syrup lends its herbal flavor to cold sodas, but could also be stirred into hot water for a soothing nighttime beverage. For a more surprising and exotic version, substitute grapefruit zest for lemon. MAKES ABOUT 1¼ CUPS

1 cup water

1 cup sugar

Pinch of salt

2 tablespoons dried or fresh chamomile

2 pieces lemon zest

¼ teaspoon citric acid solution

In a small saucepan set over medium heat, bring the water, sugar, and salt to a simmer. Add the chamomile, lemon zest, and citric acid, and steep for 20 minutes.

Strain the syrup through a fine-mesh strainer and let cool. Store the syrup in an airtight container in the refrigerator for up to 14 days.

CHAMOMILE SODA

For one drink, fill a tall glass with ice. Add 3 tablespoons of the Chamomile Syrup, top with seltzer, and mix gently.

CHAMOMILE-GRAPEFRUIT SODA

For one drink, fill a tall glass with ice. Squeeze in the juice of half a lemon. Add 1 tablespoon of the Chamomile Syrup and 2 tablespoons of Grapefruit Syrup (page 21). Top with seltzer and mix gently.

HIBISCUS SYRUP

When I vend icy-cold sodas at The New Amsterdam Market in New York City, I find more return customers looking for hibiscus soda than for any other flavor. An edible flower, hibiscus packs a concentrated flavor punch when dried and used as an ingredient in home-brewed drinks. With a nice, almost dry tartness that hints at lemon and a dazzling ruby-magenta color, hibiscus makes a fragrant and punchy tea. When rounded out with a sweetener, hibiscus is a surprising and delightful base for a great sparkling drink. The sugar and agave balance that, and the ginger adds a little heat. A friend of mine adds a dash of this to prosecco, her version of the French drink Kir Royale. MAKES ABOUT 1¼ CUPS

1 cup water

½ cup sugar

½ cup fresh lime juice

⅓ cup light agave nectar

½ tablespoon grated fresh ginger

2 tablespoons dried hibiscus flowers

In a medium saucepan set over medium heat, bring the water, sugar, lime juice, and agave to a simmer. Add the ginger and simmer for 30 minutes. Remove the pan from the heat and add the hibiscus flowers. Steep for 20 minutes.

Strain the syrup through a fine-mesh strainer, discarding the flowers, and let cool. Store in an airtight container in the refrigerator for up to 7 days.

HIBISCUS SODA

For one drink, fill a tall glass with ice. Squeeze in the juice of half a lime. Add 3 tablespoons of the Hibiscus Syrup, top with seltzer, and stir.

LUCY AND RICKY RICKEY

MAKES 1 DRINK

Each distinct and appealing alone, but made better as a team, hibiscus and lime are the Lucy and Ricky of the soda-syrup world.

2 tablespoons Hibiscus Syrup (page 70)

2 tablespoons Lime Syrup (page 23)

1 tablespoon fresh lime juice

1 teaspoon acid phosphate or citric acid solution

Seltzer

Maraschino cherry, for garnish

Lime wheel, for garnish

Fill a tall glass with ice. Pour in the hibiscus and lime syrups, lime juice, and acid phosphate. Add cold seltzer almost to the top of the glass, and mix gently. Garnish with the cherry and lime wheel.

ROSE SYRUP

The essence of rose is used throughout the world to flavor and perfume teas, desserts, and dairy drinks. I use both rose petals and rose hips for a nice floral aroma with depth. A complicated and sometimes acquired taste, Rose Syrup makes a lovely soda. You can also tip it into lemonade to conjure up the exotic cuisines of Lebanon and Israel. You can find food-grade rose petals at wholesale herb companies, at specialty tea stores, and on the Internet.

MAKES ABOUT 1 CUP

¾ cup water

½ cup sugar

1 ounce rose hips, coarsely chopped

½ ounce organic, food-grade rose petals

In a medium saucepan set over medium heat, bring the water and sugar to a simmer. Add the rose hips and petals, and remove the pan from the heat. Steep for 20 minutes.

Strain the syrup through a fine-mesh strainer and let cool. Store in an airtight container in the refrigerator for up to 14 days.

ROSE SODA

For one drink, fill a tall glass with ice. Add 3 tablespoons of the Rose Syrup, top with seltzer, and mix gently.

HRISTIA'S ROSE

MAKES 1 DRINK

I created this drink for my friends Hristo and Tia as a wedding present. Bottles of this flavored syrup—with a ribbon tied on and a label that my wife, Erica, a graphic artist, designed—were presented to celebrants as they left. Tia wanted a flavor with a floral note, and Hristo requested something deep and rich. I combined the two and came up with this drink.

3 tablespoons Dried Cherry Syrup (page 77)

¼ teaspoon citric acid solution

Seltzer

2 drops Rose Syrup (page 73)

Fill a tall glass with ice. Add the cherry syrup and citric acid. Pour in cold seltzer and mix gently. Add a couple of drops of the rose syrup and serve.

FOUNTAIN FACT

With the start of Prohibition, bartenders found themselves out of a job, so many of these people-savvy showmen usurped inexperienced teens as soda jerks, elevating the position to new, hipster status. The allure of the smartly uniformed jerk is evidenced in the 1952 film *Has Anybody Seen My Gal?* starring Rock Hudson as the smooth, capable alchemist behind the gleaming, modern taps and tools of the trade.

ORGEAT SYRUP

Relatively clear in the bottle, this predominantly almond-flavored syrup turns milky when added to water or seltzer. Like a vinaigrette, the liquid is an emulsion, which means it is a mixture of two substances that cannot fully blend—in this case, nut oil and water. Often called "French barley water," it dates back to a time when a barley-almond mixture was its base; the flavoring is still popular throughout Europe, used in sparkling water and coffee. As a base for classic cocktails, Orgeat is a component in the Mai Tai and Planter's Punch. MAKES ABOUT 2 CUPS

¾ cup blanched almonds

1 cup sugar

1 thin piece orange zest (about the size of your thumb)

1½ cups boiling water

1 scant drop orange blossom water

Combine the almonds and sugar in the bowl of a food processor and process until the nuts are coarsely chopped. Transfer the mixture to a heat-proof bowl, add the orange zest, and pour in the boiling water. Stir until the sugar is completely dissolved. Cover the bowl and refrigerate overnight.

The next day, strain the syrup through cheesecloth or a coffee filter. Stir in the orange blossom water thoroughly. Store the syrup in an airtight container in the refrigerator for up to 14 days.

ALMOND-ORANGE SODA

For one drink, fill a glass with ice. Add 2 tablespoons of Seville Orange Syrup (page 22) and 1 tablespoon of the Orgeat Syrup. Top with seltzer and garnish with an orange wheel.

DRIED CHERRY SYRUP

Dried cherries make a sublime soda, and it's fun to try making this syrup with a few different varieties. Here, I call for plump dried dark sweet cherries. You can also use dried tart red cherries, and the flavor will be a little different. When you make soda, experiment with citric acid or acid phosphate—the more you add, the brighter the flavor will be. **MAKES ABOUT 2 CUPS**

2 cups water

1 cup sugar

¾ cup dried sweet cherries

In a medium saucepan set over medium heat, bring the water, sugar, and dried cherries to a boil. Remove the pan from the heat and steep for 2 hours.

Using a stick blender, break up the cherries until the mixture is chunky (don't blend it smooth). If you don't have a stick blender, you can use a fork or potato masher to smash them. Strain the syrup through a fine-mesh strainer, discard the cherries, and let cool. Store the syrup in an airtight container in the refrigerator for up to 14 days.

CHERRY SODA

For one drink, fill a tall glass with ice. Add 3 table-spoons of the Dried Cherry Syrup and a few dashes of citric acid solution or acid phosphate. Top with seltzer and mix gently.

LOVAGE SYRUP

Many people have asked me, "What does lovage taste like?" When I tell them the flavor closely resembles celery, they usually seem unsure how to take that. Lovage is an herb. Its leaves are often used in salads, and the root can be eaten as a vegetable. Widely used in kitchens all over the world, lovage has also become popular as an addition to cocktails in bars and restaurants, and it's now fairly easy to find through wholesale herb companies, on the Internet, and in stores stocking bulk herbs and teas. It's a natural as a flavor in cocktails. The Modern, the restaurant in the Museum of Modern Art, in New York City, serves a traditional Negroni made with lovage syrup. As you might imagine, the syrup is also a nice addition to a Bloody Mary.

MAKES ABOUT 2½ CUPS

---

2 cups water

1¾ cups sugar

Pinch of salt

1 tablespoon dried lovage root

½ tablespoon dried lovage leaf

Juice of 1 lemon

In a medium saucepan set over medium heat, bring the water, sugar, and salt to a boil. Remove the pan from the heat and add the lovage root and leaf. Steep for about 45 minutes.

Strain the syrup through a fine-mesh strainer and discard the solids. Add the lemon juice and let cool. Store in an airtight container in the refrigerator for up to 7 days.

LOVAGE SODA

For one drink, fill a tall glass with ice. Add 3 tablespoons of the Lovage Syrup, top with seltzer, and mix gently.

GINGER RAISIN
SHRUB SYRUP

The spicy warmth of ginger marries beautifully with the honeyed-syrup flavor of the golden raisins in this recipe. Blended with the tart and fruity apple cider vinegar, this syrup pops when added to seltzer, blooming into a tangy and fresh soda unlike any commercially bottled drink. Pair this soda with a corned beef on rye with mustard or a feta-topped salad. MAKES ABOUT 2 CUPS

1 cup apple cider vinegar

½ cup water

¾ cup sugar

Pinch of salt

¼ cup golden raisins

1 tablespoon grated fresh ginger

In a medium saucepan set over medium heat, bring the vinegar, water, sugar, and salt to a boil. Remove the pan from the heat and add the raisins and ginger. Cover the pan and steep at room temperature for 24 hours.

The next day, smash the raisins with a fork or potato masher. Strain the syrup through a fine-mesh strainer. Store the syrup in an airtight container in the refrigerator for up to 14 days.

GINGER RAISIN SHRUB

For one drink, fill a tall glass with ice. Add 3 tablespoons of the Ginger Raisin Shrub Syrup, top with seltzer, and stir.

BLUEBERRY AND STAR ANISE SHRUB SYRUP

All shrubs are considered to have health-boosting properties, but this one offers an extra jolt from exotic star anise. With a flavor familiar to many from the liqueurs Galliano and Sambuca, star anise is also widely used in Chinese cuisine, as an ingredient in five-spice powder, and in Indian cooking, as a major component of the spice blend garam masala. In traditional Asian medicine, it's considered a warming spice and is useful in curing colds; today, one of its chemical elements (shikimic acid) is used in the over-the-counter influenza remedy Tamiflu. Here, the sweet, ripe fullness of the blueberries balances out the strong, one-note licorice taste of the star anise, resulting in a smooth, fresh-tasting soda with just a hint of herb. **MAKES ABOUT 3 CUPS**

1½ cups water

1 cup sugar

1½ cups fresh blueberries

¾ cup red wine vinegar

2 star anise

In a medium saucepan set over medium heat, bring the water and sugar to a boil. Put the blueberries, vinegar, and star anise in a large heatproof bowl. Pour the boiling liquid over the ingredients in the bowl, cover, and steep for 20 minutes.

Carefully mash the blueberries with a fork or potato masher and let cool. Transfer the mixture, covered, to the refrigerator and chill for 2 days to allow the flavors to blend before use.

When ready to use, strain the syrup through a fine-mesh strainer and discard the solids. Store the syrup in an airtight container in the refrigerator for up to 14 days.

BLUEBERRY AND STAR ANISE SHRUB

For one drink, fill a tall glass with ice. Add 3 tablespoons of the Blueberry and Star Anise Shrub Syrup, top with seltzer, and mix gently.

SHRUBS |
An old-school type of drink, the shrub is a vinegar-based beverage that is usually lightly sweetened and flavored with fruit. Vinegar drinks have long been drunk for health reasons. As early as 400 B.C., ancient Greeks were quaffing natural apple cider vinegar sweetened with honey to cure everything from lethargy to sallow skin. Modern shrubs have enough vinegar to taste tart and are never cloyingly sweet, so you can drink them without worrying about consuming a lot of sugar. In colonial times, settlers spiked them with brandy or rum. Today, shrubs can be found on upscale, fashionable restaurant menus.

RASPBERRY–DRIED APRICOT SHRUB SYRUP

Apricot and raspberry are two fruits that go hand in hand as a flavor combo. Apricot's rich sweetness and the tangy zing of raspberries are often combined to make jams, sauces, salad dressings, baked goods, and even sangria. For this syrup, the mildly spicy pink peppercorns—exotic, but never over the top—bring out the flavor of the fruits, the way black pepper enhances already-present tastes. MAKES ABOUT 3 CUPS

2 cups water

1¼ cups sugar

Pinch of salt

1¼ cups fresh raspberries

½ cup dried apricots, halved

¾ cup champagne vinegar

10 pink peppercorns

In a medium saucepan set over medium heat, bring the water, sugar, and salt to a boil. Remove the pan from the heat and add the raspberries, apricots, vinegar, and peppercorns. Cover the pan and steep at room temperature for 24 hours.

The next day, smash the raspberries and apricots with a fork or potato masher. Strain the syrup through a fine-mesh strainer and discard the solids. Store in an airtight container in the refrigerator for up to 14 days.

RASPBERRY–DRIED APRICOT SHRUB

For one drink, fill a tall glass with ice. Add 3 tablespoons of the Raspberry–Dried Apricot Shrub Syrup, top with seltzer, and mix gently.

DRIED FIG SHRUB SYRUP

Sweet and succulent, figs are considered one of the oldest cultivated fruit crops on record, along with olives and grapes, and they enjoy popularity from the Middle East, to the Mediterranean, to the United States. If you find fresh figs at your gourmet food market or specialty store, go ahead and substitute them for dried, but double the amount. Serve this soda with a platter of mixed olives and goat cheese. The strong, salty tastes will complement the fig and vinegar flavors. **MAKES ABOUT 3 CUPS**

---

2 cups water

1½ cups sugar

1 cup red wine vinegar

8 dried figs, cut in half

1 cinnamon stick

4 whole cloves

In a medium saucepan set over medium heat, bring the water and sugar to a boil. Put the vinegar, figs, cinnamon stick, and cloves in a large heatproof bowl. Carefully pour the boiling liquid over the figs and spices. Cover the bowl and let cool. Refrigerate for 2 days to allow the flavors to blend.

When you're ready to use, strain the syrup through a fine-mesh strainer and discard the solids. Store the syrup in an airtight container in the refrigerator for up to 14 days.

DRIED FIG SHRUB

For one drink, fill a tall glass with ice. Add 3 tablespoons of the Dried Fig Shrub Syrup, top with seltzer, and mix gently.

EGG CREAMS, EGG SHAKES, AND ICE CREAM SODAS

CLASSIC CHOCOLATE EGG CREAM

The name egg cream is misleading—in actuality, the soda fountain classic contains no eggs and no cream. The three winning elements are milk, flavored syrup, and seltzer. For an icy beverage like top soda jerks used to craft, it's best to frost glasses in the freezer. See page 90 for tips on making the best egg cream. MAKES 1 DRINK

½ cup whole milk

Seltzer

4 tablespoons Chocolate Syrup (page 56)

Pour the milk into a very cold 12-ounce glass. Slowly pour in the seltzer, then gently add the syrup. Using a long spoon, stir well and serve.

STEP IT UP

- Make a Classic Vanilla Egg Cream by substituting Vanilla Syrup (page 57) for the Chocolate Syrup.
- Make a Classic Coffee Egg Cream by substituting Coffee Syrup (page 62) for the Chocolate Syrup.

BUILDING THE PERFECT EGG CREAM, MY WAY

There's some debate as to what is the best method for making an egg cream. Arguments arise about the ingredients and the order in which they're layered, the size of the glass, and the length of the spoon. There are even disagreements about the birth of the egg cream, though most beverage historians think that it was created in Brooklyn in the 1920s. Some like it mixed up flat, dark, and rich. I like it simple and frothy, hinting at a milkshake but lighter. The carbonation should be the star. This is my tried-and-true technique.

1 Use full-fat milk for richness. This is an occasional treat. Enjoy it to the fullest!

2 Keep it cold—chill your ingredients and equipment: syrup, milk, seltzer, and glass.

3 Put the milk in the glass first. It should be about as high as 2 fingers from the bottom of your glass.

4 Add the seltzer, very slowly, until the foam starts to reach the top—be careful that it doesn't run over.

5 Pour in the syrup and, quickly but lightly, stir well, using a long spoon to reach the bottom of the glass, until the entire drink is blended.

MALAYSIAN EGG CREAM

One of Malaysia's favorite drinks is the bandung. An adaptation of the rose milk served in India, bandung consists of rose cordial syrup mixed with milk. I've adopted the idea and given it a New York twist with the addition of seltzer, creating a cousin to the Asian refresher. See facing page for tips on making the best egg cream. **MAKES 1 DRINK**

½ cup ice-cold whole milk

Seltzer

2 tablespoons Rose Syrup (page 73)

Pour the milk into a very cold, tall glass. Slowly pour in the seltzer and, while briskly stirring, pour in the rose syrup. Stir until the syrup is dissolved and serve.

SPICED MAPLE
EGG CREAM

This concoction will lull your taste buds with its cool creaminess of milk and comforting sweetness of maple. It's a great drink first thing in the morning or for autumn evenings in front of the fire. See page 90 for tips on making the best egg cream. **MAKES 1 DRINK**

½ cup whole milk

Seltzer

4 tablespoons Spiced Maple Syrup (page 68)

Pour the milk into a very cold, tall glass. Slowly pour in the seltzer, then gently add the syrup. Using a long spoon, stir well and serve.

CANDY CAP MUSHROOM AND TOASTED ALMOND EGG CREAM

A rich, earthy treat, this recipe was inspired by a dessert I had in San Francisco and by a fascinating mushroom forager who shared her knowledge with me. See page 90 for tips on making the best egg cream. MAKES 1 DRINK

½ cup Candy Cap Milk (recipe follows)

Seltzer

3 tablespoons Toasted Almond Syrup (page 59)

Pour the milk into a very cold, tall glass. Slowly pour in the seltzer, then gently add the syrup. Using a long spoon, stir well and serve.

CANDY CAP MILK

MAKES 1 QUART

2 large pieces dried candy cap mushrooms (see Sources, page 141)

1 quart whole milk

1 tablespoon maple sugar (see Sources, page 141)

Grind the mushrooms in a spice grinder or with a mortar and pestle until reduced to a powder. Put the powder in a container that can be sealed airtight and add the milk and maple sugar. Shake well and refrigerate overnight to allow the flavors to blend.

The milk will keep in the refrigerator for the length of the original milk's shelf life.

GRANDPA ANTHONY'S
CHERRY CREAM SODA

This drink is a tribute to my grandpa, who shared his secret sweets with my brother and me, even when Grandma was fussing over his diet and laying down the law. Happily, the occasional can of black cherry soda poured into tall glasses of milk, with a few black licorice pieces on the side, never harmed his diabetes. It brought a lot of sweetness to the life of the old man and his two favorite little buddies. **MAKES 1 DRINK**

3 tablespoons Sour Cherry Syrup (page 32) or Dried Cherry Syrup (page 77)

Seltzer

3 tablespoons whole milk

Fill a tall glass with ice. Add the syrup, pour in the seltzer until the glass is almost full, and stir. Top with the milk and serve.

CHOCOLATE MALT
EGG SHAKE

Eager to dissociate from its origins as a whiskey-based drink shaken with a raw egg, the egg shake has changed its reputation, becoming a soda-fountain favorite for the whole family. In a bid to rebrand it, the "virgin" treat was called "a wholesome drink, made with chocolate, vanilla, or strawberry." As a kid, I loved Orange Julius, the fast-food restaurant featuring a cold, frothy drink made with orange juice that could be ordered with or without the egg. I always chose with the egg because of how it made the sweet drink more substantial and creamier. That's what I love about egg shakes, and if you're careful with your sourcing, raw eggs shouldn't pose a problem. MAKES 1 DRINK

1 whole large egg

2 tablespoons heavy cream

4 tablespoons Chocolate Syrup (page 56)

1 tablespoon malted milk powder

Seltzer

In a cocktail shaker, shake the egg until it's frothy. Put 1 or 2 ice cubes in the shaker, add the cream, and shake for about 15 seconds. Add the syrup and malt powder, and shake one final time. Pour in the seltzer until the foam comes to the top of the shaker, then pour the mixture back and forth from shaker to shaker a couple of times until well combined. Pour into a tall glass and serve.

THE CLASSIC METHOD FOR THE PERFECT EGG SHAKE

In the late nineteenth century, soda fountains served milkshakes that featured ice cream or heavy sweet cream and a whole fresh egg. However, wartime rationing and soda fountain taxation resulted in the elimination of these high-cost dairy ingredients, giving rise to the thinner egg cream. For a thick and creamy old-fashioned egg shake, it's important to follow my method to a tee. Here are some tips for creating the best drink every time.

1 Crack a cold whole egg into a cocktail shaker and shake vigorously for 5 seconds.

2 Add 2 ice cubes and the cream and shake for another 15 seconds.

3 Add the syrup and shake for another 10 seconds.

4 Remove the small shaker, and add the seltzer to the shaken mixture until the foam is about three-fourths of the way up the big shaker. Pour the mixture into the small shaker, then back into the large shaker.

5 Put the rim of the shaker on the rim of your serving glass and slowly pour the egg shake into the glass while slowly lifting the shaker.

GINGER EGG SHAKE

This is one of my favorite egg shakes because I love the contrast of the sharp, warm spice with the smooth, creamy coldness. It's actually really great for breakfast or to serve with spicy Vietnamese or Thai dishes. See page 97 for tips on making the best egg shake. MAKES 1 DRINK

1 whole large egg

2 tablespoons heavy cream

4 tablespoons Ginger Syrup (page 27)

Seltzer

In a cocktail shaker, shake the egg until it's frothy. Put 1 or 2 ice cubes in the shaker, add the cream, and shake for about 15 seconds. Add the syrup and shake one final time. Pour in the seltzer until the foam comes to the top of the shaker, then pour the mixture back and forth from shaker to shaker a couple of times until well combined. Pour into a tall glass and serve.

BANANA GUAVA EGG SHAKE

If I were lounging on a deck in The Islands, relaxing in the warm sun, staring out at the crystal-blue water, this is the drink I'd want at my elbow. See page 97 for tips on making the best egg shake. MAKES 1 DRINK

1 whole large egg

2 tablespoons heavy cream

3 tablespoons Banana Syrup (page 49)

1 tablespoon Guava Syrup (page 28)

Seltzer

In a cocktail shaker, shake the egg until it's frothy. Put 1 or 2 ice cubes in the shaker, add the cream, and shake for about 15 seconds. Add the syrups and shake one final time. Pour in the seltzer until the foam comes to the top of the shaker, then pour the mixture back and forth from shaker to shaker a couple of times until well combined. Pour into a tall glass and serve.

LEMON EGG SHAKE

Lemon as an ingredient brightens and hones the flavor of any recipe. I love the combination of tart and creamy in this egg shake recipe. The citrusy flavor gives a lift to the richness of the cream, making this a satisfying and substantial drink. See page 97 for tips on making the best egg shake.

MAKES 1 DRINK

---

1 whole large egg

2 tablespoons heavy cream

4 tablespoons Lemon Syrup (page 23)

1 tablespoon fresh lemon juice

Seltzer

In a cocktail shaker, shake the egg until it's frothy. Put 1 or 2 ice cubes in the shaker, add the cream, and shake for about 15 seconds. Add the syrup and juice and shake one final time. Pour in the seltzer until the foam comes to the top of the shaker, then pour the mixture back and forth from shaker to shaker a couple of times until well combined. Pour into a tall glass and serve.

OLD-FASHIONED ICE CREAM SODAS

Ice cream sodas bring back so many memories of afternoons spent at the soda fountain when I was a kid. Most people instantly recognize two of the most popular in this dessert category: the Coke float and the root beer float. I think the best classic ice cream soda is the Classic Black and White (recipe follows). But my favorite thing about these drinks is how versatile they are. In the recipes here, I've mixed and matched some of my sodas with unique ice creams, and I hope the recipes encourage you to try your own flavor combinations.

The key to a great ice cream soda is to position the ice cream properly. If it extends way down into the seltzer, the foam will overflow. If it's too high on the rim, you won't get any of that wonderful, rich soda foam. Here's my technique for making the very best ice cream soda:

1 Start with a tall, frosty glass—a footed, tulip-shaped soda glass works best, if you have it.

2 Measure 3 or 4 tablespoonfuls of your favorite syrup and drizzle it down the sides of the glass.

3 Slowly pour in the seltzer to about 3 fingers below the top.

4 Take a good-size scoop of your favorite ice cream and secure it on the rim by pressing the ball of ice cream down firmly, and only releasing it from its scoop when it's halfway sunk and anchored. This will leave a gap into which the foam can expand.

5 Serve with a bendy straw and a long-handled spoon. For extra authenticity, add a dollop of whipped cream and a maraschino cherry.

CLASSIC
BLACK AND WHITE

A traditional milkshake recipe, the classic version calls for a blend of creamy vanilla ice cream and rich chocolate syrup. Some people think vanilla ice cream represents a lack of flavor, since most ice creams are blended with fruit, sauce, or add-ins. But the characteristic, practically indescribable flavor of pure vanilla pops in my creamy concoction, rich with the tiny flecks that identify it as all natural. See facing page for tips on making the best ice cream soda.

MAKES 1 DRINK

---

4 tablespoons Chocolate Syrup (page 56)

Seltzer

1 scoop Vanilla Ice Cream (recipe follows)

Fill a tall glass with ice. Add the syrup. Add enough seltzer until the glass is two-thirds full, stirring briskly. Add the ice cream, then top with more seltzer, taking care that it doesn't run over.

VANILLA ICE CREAM

MAKES 1 QUART

$1\frac{1}{2}$ cups half-and-half

1 cup sugar

1 vanilla bean, halved

3 large egg yolks

$\frac{3}{4}$ cup heavy cream

Fill a large bowl with ice and set aside.

In a medium saucepan set over medium-high heat, combine the half-and-half and $\frac{3}{4}$ cup of the sugar. Scrape the seeds out of the vanilla bean and add the seeds and pod to the pan. Remove the pan from the heat and steep for 20 minutes.

In a large bowl, whisk together the eggs and the remaining $\frac{1}{4}$ cup sugar. Bring the half-and-half back to a steady simmer. While whisking the eggs constantly, slowly pour in the hot half-and-half. Whisk until well combined, then pour the mixture back into the saucepan. Cook over medium heat until the liquid has thickened and coats the back of a spoon, about 5 minutes.

Strain the custard through a fine-mesh strainer into a clean bowl, and set it over the bowl of ice to cool. When cool, add the cream. Refrigerate overnight.

The next day, process the custard in your ice cream machine according to the manufacturer's instructions. The ice cream will keep in an airtight container in the freezer for 14 days.

PEACH-CHAMOMILE
ICE CREAM SODA

Peaches are tricky. A bad peach—mealy, dry, flavorless—isn't worth eating. Good peaches, on the other hand, like the ones you get in Georgia or South Carolina, with skins that pop like balloons and juice that drips down to your neck, well, that's a thing of beauty. Chamomile's delicate flavor is complemented by the bright sweetness of the peaches in this recipe. Both prized for fragrance, peaches and chamomile are winning partners in a beverage. See page 102 for tips on making the best ice cream soda. **MAKES 1 DRINK**

3 tablespoons Chamomile Syrup (page 69)

Seltzer

1 scoop Peach Ice Cream (recipe follows)

Fill a tall glass with ice. Add the syrup. Add enough seltzer until the glass is two-thirds full, stirring briskly. Add the ice cream, then top with more seltzer, taking care that it doesn't run over.

PEACH ICE CREAM

MAKES ABOUT 3 CUPS

1 pound fresh, ripe peaches, skinned and pitted

Pinch of salt

⅔ cup sugar

1¼ cups whole milk

4 large egg yolks

1¼ cups heavy cream

Put the peaches in a large saucepan with the salt and ⅓ cup of the sugar. Cook on low heat for 5 minutes to draw out and reduce some of the liquid. Transfer to a bowl and put in the refrigerator to cool, about 30 minutes. Puree in a blender or food mill and return to the bowl.

Fill a large bowl with ice and set aside. Put the milk and the remaining ⅓ cup sugar into a medium saucepan set over medium-high heat, and bring to a steady simmer.

In a medium bowl, whisk the eggs until they are light yellow, about 1 minute. While whisking, slowly pour in the hot milk mixture. Whisk well, then pour the mixture back into the saucepan. Cook over medium heat until the liquid coats the back of a spoon, about 5 minutes.

Strain the custard over the peaches and put the bowl into the bowl of ice. Stir in the cream, chill for about 30 minutes, and refrigerate overnight.

The next day, process the peach custard in your ice cream machine according to the manufacturer's instructions. The ice cream will keep in an airtight container in the freezer for 14 days.

QUINCE AND GOAT CHEESE
ICE CREAM SODA

Everyone loves a sweet and salty snack, and this sophisticated beverage hits a perfect balance. The sweet-tart flavor of the quince and the creamy texture and saltiness of the cheese make a perfect pair in this dessert. See page 102 for tips on making the best ice cream soda. MAKES 1 DRINK

4 tablespoons Quince Syrup (page 48)

Seltzer

1 scoop Goat Cheese Ice Cream (recipe follows)

Fill a tall glass with ice. Add the syrup. Add enough seltzer until the glass is two-thirds full, stirring briskly. Add the ice cream, then top with more seltzer, taking care that it doesn't run over.

Robert Green is credited with inventing the first ice cream soda, in 1874. Legend has it that the vendor began his day at the Franklin Institute's semi-centennial celebration in Philadelphia by selling a concoction of cream, syrup, and seltzer. He ran out of cream and improvised with vanilla ice cream, increasing his sales for the day by tenfold!

GOAT CHEESE ICE CREAM

MAKES ABOUT 3 CUPS

8 ounces (1 cup) fresh goat cheese

⅔ cup sugar

Pinch of salt

1 cup whole milk

6 large egg yolks

½ cup heavy cream

Break up the goat cheese in a medium bowl and set aside. Fill a large bowl with ice and set aside.

In a medium saucepan set over medium-high heat, combine ⅓ cup of the sugar, the salt, and the milk, and bring to a steady simmer, about 5 minutes.

Meanwhile, in a separate medium bowl, whisk together the eggs and the remaining ⅓ cup sugar. Beat for 1 minute until the mixture is a light yellow. While whisking the eggs constantly, slowly pour in the hot milk mixture. Whisk until well combined, then pour the mixture back into the saucepan. Cook over medium heat until the liquid has thickened and coats the back of a spoon, about 5 minutes.

Pour the hot custard into the bowl of goat cheese and stir until the cheese is melted. Strain through a fine-mesh strainer into a clean bowl and put it into the bowl of ice to cool. While it cools, add the cream. Refrigerate overnight.

The next day, process the custard in your ice cream machine according to the manufacturer's instructions. The ice cream will keep in an airtight container in the freezer for 14 days.

CHERRY VERBENA
ICE CREAM SODA

With the crisp, tangy flavor of cherries and the herbal-citrus taste of lemon verbena, this cool treat will make any summer celebration more special. Unexpected and fresh, this delicate ice cream pairs well with tart and tangy flavors. It's delicious served with a dessert wine with a cherry finish, or alongside a bowl of fresh berries. See page 102 for tips on making the best ice cream soda. **MAKES 1 DRINK**

3 tablespoons Sour Cherry Syrup (page 32) or Dried Cherry Syrup (page 77)

Seltzer

1 scoop Lemon Verbena Ice Cream (recipe follows)

Fill a tall glass with ice. Add the syrup. Add enough seltzer until the glass is two-thirds full, stirring briskly. Add the ice cream, then top with more seltzer, taking care that it doesn't run over.

LEMON VERBENA ICE CREAM

MAKES ABOUT 3 CUPS

1 cup whole milk

Pinch of salt

$^{3}\!/_{4}$ cup sugar

1 bunch lemon verbena

5 large egg yolks

1 tablespoon fresh lemon juice

2 cups heavy cream

In a medium saucepan set over low heat, combine the milk, salt, and $^{1}\!/_{2}$ cup of the sugar. Heat for about 5 minutes, until warm. Remove the pan from the heat, add the lemon verbena, and steep for 15 minutes.

Fill a large bowl with ice and set aside.

In a medium bowl, whisk together the remaining $^{1}\!/_{4}$ cup sugar and the eggs. Bring the milk back to a simmer. While whisking the eggs, slowly pour in the hot milk mixture. Whisk well and pour the mixture back into the saucepan. Cook over medium heat until the liquid has thickened and coats the back of a spoon, 5 minutes.

Strain the custard into a clean bowl, set it into the bowl of ice, add the lemon juice, and let cool. Add the cream when completely cool. Refrigerate overnight.

The next day, process the custard in your ice cream machine according to the manufacturer's instructions. The ice cream will keep in an airtight container in the freezer for 14 days.

ANISE HYSSOP AND STRAWBERRY ICE CREAM SODA

This is a drink from my fantasy soda fountain. These flavors together remind me of my favorite candies. The fruity-fresh strawberry and the spicy licorice note from the anise hyssop make an unusual combo that's truly delicious. See page 102 for tips on making the best ice cream soda. MAKES 1 DRINK

3 tablespoons Anise Hyssop Syrup (page 39)

Seltzer

1 scoop Strawberry Ice Cream (recipe follows)

Fill a tall glass with ice. Add the syrup. Add enough seltzer until the glass is two-thirds full, stirring briskly. Add the ice cream, then top with more seltzer, taking care that it doesn't run over.

STRAWBERRY ICE CREAM

MAKES 1 QUART

3 cups strawberries, hulled

1½ cups half-and-half

Pinch of salt

½ cup sugar

4 large egg yolks

¾ cup heavy cream

1 ounce vodka or other spirit of your choice

FOUNTAIN FACT

Still popular during the two world wars, soda fountains were considered essential for soldiers' morale. During World War I, soda fountains were installed on some navy ships, and during World War II, they were often associated with USO clubs, army post exchanges, and Red Cross centers.

Puree the strawberries in a blender or food mill. Pour into a large bowl and set aside. Fill a large bowl with ice and set aside.

In a medium saucepan set over medium heat, combine the half-and-half, salt, and ¼ cup of the sugar and bring to a simmer, 5 minutes.

In a medium bowl, whisk together the eggs and remaining ¼ cup sugar. While whisking the eggs, slowly pour in the hot mixture. Whisk well and pour the mixture back into the saucepan. Cook over medium heat until the liquid has thickened and coats the back of a spoon, 5 minutes.

Strain the custard over the strawberry puree, put the bowl into the bowl of ice, and let cool. Add the cream and vodka. Refrigerate overnight.

The next day, process the custard in your ice cream machine according to the manufacturer's instructions. The ice cream will keep in an airtight container in the freezer for 14 days.

COCKTAILS

SARSAPARILLA JACK

With the sweet kick of sippin' whiskey and the old-fashioned flavor of horehound candy, this is the perfect cocktail for a summer lawn party or Kentucky Derby fete. The woody notes of the whiskey and the earthy notes of the sarsaparilla blend beautifully, and the whole combo is lightened up with a hint of mint. **MAKES 1 DRINK**

1½ ounces whiskey, such as Jack Daniel's

1 tablespoon Sarsaparilla Syrup (page 58)

3 fresh mint leaves

Seltzer

Lime wedge, for garnish

Fresh mint leaf, for garnish

Combine the whiskey, syrup, and mint leaves in a cocktail shaker and fill with ice. Shake until chilled, then strain into a lowball (old-fashioned) glass filled with ice. Top with the seltzer, garnish with the lime wedge and mint leaf, and serve.

TEQUILA SUNRISE

A nostalgic favorite, the Tequila Sunrise is like an old friend. In my youth, it was my go-to drink for kicking back and relaxing with friends—and on occasion, I'll admit, for raising a little hell. MAKES 1 DRINK

½ cup orange juice

2 ounces tequila

2 tablespoons Pomegranate Syrup (page 33)

Measure the orange juice and tequila into a Collins glass filled with ice. Carefully float the syrup on the top to execute the traditional, gorgeous color combination.

THE FALL (AND RISE!) OF THE TRADITIONAL SODA FOUNTAIN

From the 1940s to the 1960s, the popularity of traditional brick-and-mortar soda fountains declined in America. As automobile culture boomed many families settled in the spacious suburbs, leaving main-street culture behind. With the growing economy, America's work habits changed and people embraced the quick lunches of drive-ins and car-hop burger joints, making a switch from drugstore lunch counters. Lastly, the invention of vending machines, along with canned and bottled sodas, meant that soft-drink lovers could now serve themselves, anytime and anyplace. For a brief period in time, the few American soda fountains that remained became curiosities.

The last decade has welcomed a resurrection of the classic soda fountain. A desire for the simple ways of the past along with a newfound desire for purity and freshness has enlivened old soda fountains and laid the groundwork for new ones. Soda drinkers are flocking to fountains for fresh, delicious, handcrafted sodas and drinks. Long live the soda fountain!

BITTER LEMON REFRESHER

For those who prefer a less sweet cocktail but love the tangy taste of lemon, this alternative to a Lemon Drop or an Arnold Palmer hits the mark. The combination of cooked and fresh Meyer lemon lends just the right hint of bitterness and sweet-tart freshness. MAKES 1 DRINK

2 tablespoons syrup from Eight-Hour Meyer Lemons in Syrup (page 50)

1½ ounces vodka

Juice of ½ Meyer lemon

Seltzer

Strip of the cooked lemon, for garnish

Fill a rocks glass with ice. Pour in the syrup, vodka, and lemon juice, and stir. Top with the seltzer, garnish with a slice of the cooked lemon, and serve.

LOVAGE GIN FIZZ

Hendrick's is an unusual, limited-production Scottish gin that balances the flavors of cucumber and rose with the traditional juniper. I especially like the fact that it's bottled in an old-fashioned brown, apothecary-style bottle. It has a unique flavor and is the best liquor for this cocktail, but if it's not available, Bombay Sapphire or another quality gin will do nicely. MAKES 1 DRINK

2 ounces Hendrick's gin

2 tablespoons Lovage Syrup (page 78)

2 tablespoons fresh lime juice

Seltzer

Celery stalk, for garnish

Fill a Collins glass with ice. Pour in the gin, syrup, and lime juice. Top with the seltzer, and stir. Serve with a stalk of celery.

CEL-RAY TONIC

Most serious soda drinkers know of Dr. Brown's Cel-Ray Tonic—and most either hate it or love it, with very little in between. The vegetal, slightly zingy drink with a flavor ever so slightly reminiscent of ginger ale was so popular with Jewish immigrants in the 1930s—partly owing to the belief that it was a medicinal elixir—that it earned the nickname "Jewish Champagne." It retained a loyal following long after the U.S. Food and Drug Administration forbade the company to call the drink a "tonic," forcing a name change to "soda."

CLOVER CLUB

The Clover Club is a cocktail lover's cocktail, predating Prohibition and making it one of the true classics. Pale pink, foamy, and beautiful in an up glass, this cocktail began as a gentleman's drink, named after a Philadelphia men's club whose members included captains of industry and business titans. Despite its appearance, the drink packs a punch. MAKES 1 DRINK

1 egg white

1½ ounces gin

½ tablespoon Pomegranate Syrup (page 33)

1 teaspoon fresh lemon juice

Chill a small wine glass or Champagne coupe. Shake the egg white in a chilled cocktail shaker for about 5 minutes. Add several ice cubes along with the rest of the ingredients and shake again for 15 seconds. Strain into your chilled glass, and serve.

MOSCOW MULE

Another classic drink, the Moscow Mule is the Russian-themed version of the "Mule," or "Buck," cocktail, using vodka as its base liquor. My ginger syrup has extra heat, mimicking the spicier ginger beer that modern bartenders like to use for this recipe, along with lime, upping the citrus quotient. MAKES 1 DRINK

1½ ounces vodka

3 tablespoons fresh lime juice

3 tablespoons Ginger Syrup (page 27)

Seltzer

Lime wedge, for garnish

Fresh mint leaf, for garnish

Fill a highball glass or a traditional Moscow Mule copper mug one-third full with ice. Pour in the vodka, lime juice, and syrup. Top with the seltzer, garnish with the lime wedge and mint leaf, and serve.

CLASSIC
JAPANESE COCKTAIL

This is a lot like an Old-Fashioned, but with a nutty, full-bodied twist. Interestingly, though it's called a Japanese Cocktail, you might notice that the ingredients are mainly French. According to Paul Clarke's blog *The Cocktail Chronicles,* the drink was created by cookbook author and bartender Jerry Thomas in 1860 in honor of a visit to New York City by the Japanese delegation. **MAKES 1 DRINK**

2 ounces brandy

1 tablespoon Orgeat Syrup (page 76)

2 dashes of angostura bitters

Thin strip of lemon zest, for garnish

In the large half of a cocktail shaker, combine the brandy, syrup, and bitters. Fill with ice cubes and stir until chilled. Strain into a cocktail glass and garnish with a lemon twist.

GIN GIMLET

An eternal classic, the gimlet is made with gin or vodka, lime juice, and a splash of soda. Both sharp and sweet, gimlets go down easy when ice cold, and can pack a wallop, despite their delicate, pale, frothy look. If 007 weren't a martini man, I'd offer him one of these. Some craft this drink using Rose's lime juice, but I like it the fresh way, as it's more tart. Bracing and chest-warming, this very masculine cocktail should be in every man's cocktail cache. **MAKES 1 DRINK**

2 ounces gin

3 tablespoons fresh lime juice

½ tablespoon Lime Syrup (page 23)

Thin strip of lime zest, for garnish

Combine the gin, lime juice, and syrup in a cocktail shaker and fill with ice. Shake for 15 seconds and strain into a chilled martini glass. Garnish with a lime twist and serve.

KUMQUAT, ST-GERMAIN, AND PROSECCO

I'd recommend this as a replacement for Champagne at a wedding toast. The fragrant elderflower essence and prosecco's bright bubbles, along with the kumquat's association with luck, make this a terrific cocktail for celebration.

MAKES 1 DRINK

---

2 Candied Kumquats (page 52)

1 teaspoon syrup from Candied Kumquats

¾ ounce St-Germain elderflower liqueur

Chilled prosecco

In a Champagne flute or Champagne coupe, gently crush the kumquats with the back of a spoon until they burst and release their juices. Add the syrup and St-Germain, then top with prosecco and serve.

BOURBON AND CHERRY
CHOCOLATE

Good whiskey calls to mind wood smoke, maple syrup, and dark winter fruit. Add the ripe berry flavor of sour cherries and the richness of chocolate, and you have a complex and delicious drink that's sure to surprise. A treat to sip, this cocktail is warm all the way down. You can easily find chocolate bitters at better beverage and liquor stores, craft-brewing supply houses, upscale gourmet food shops, or on the Internet. It's a fun cocktail ingredient to have on hand for a range of unique drink experiments. MAKES 1 DRINK

1¾ ounces Maker's Mark bourbon

1 tablespoon Sour Cherry Syrup (page 32)

Dash of chocolate bitters

Add all the ingredients to a cocktail shaker half-filled with ice. Shake and strain over fresh ice cubes or into a rocks glass, or serve neat in a martini glass.

EGG NOG EGG SHAKE

Every year, I can't wait for the holiday season to roll around so I can enjoy the creamy, pungent flavor of spiced egg nog. The mulling spices and the earthy sweetness of maple in the Spiced Maple Syrup are the perfect flavor booster for the cream and spirits. I chose brandy and rum for this recipe.

MAKES 1 DRINK

1 large egg

2 tablespoons heavy cream

1 ounce brandy

½ ounce dark rum

2 tablespoons Spiced Maple Syrup (page 68)

Freshly grated nutmeg

Seltzer

Shake the egg in a cocktail shaker for 5 seconds. Add 2 ice cubes and the cream, and shake for 10 more seconds. Add the brandy, rum, syrup, and a few gratings of nutmeg, and shake for 10 more seconds. Pour in the seltzer until the foam reaches the top of the mixing cup, and pour the drink into a chilled serving glass. Grate fresh nutmeg on the top and serve.

HOT DRINKS

CHOCOLATE TEA
WITH MINT SYRUP

The outer shell of the cocoa bean is called the chocolate husk. These are discarded by chocolate makers and recycled as mulch or as a tea product, the latter steeped in boiling water. Made into tea, the husk yields a hot beverage with a lightly rich chocolate flavor and aroma. It can be sweetened with your choice of the syrups in this book, but I like mine best with mint. It reminds me of a smooth, hot York Peppermint Pattie. You can get chocolate husks from chocolate roasters and from wholesale-supply tea companies like SerendipiTea (see Sources, page 141). MAKES 1 DRINK

1 cup water

½ ounce chocolate husks

½ teaspoon Mint Syrup (page 38)

Fresh mint leaf, for garnish

In a small saucepan, bring the water to a boil. Remove the pan from the heat and add the chocolate husks. Steep for 5 minutes, then strain through a fine-mesh strainer into a cup. Stir in the syrup, garnish with a fresh mint leaf, and serve.

HOT LEMON SOOTHER

The snappy zing of the lemon, combined with the warming, peppery ginger, clears the head and calms the nerves. This comforting beverage is perfect for taking the chill off of a dark winter's night. MAKES 1 DRINK

¹⁄₂ tablespoon Ginger Syrup (page 27)

1 tablespoon Lemon Syrup (page 23)

¹⁄₂ tablespoon fresh lemon juice

1 cup boiling water

Lemon wedge, for garnish

Combine the syrups and lemon juice in a large mug. Fill to the top with the boiling water. Garnish with the lemon wedge and serve.

HOT APPLE SPICE CUP

This drink smells like there's a baked apple in your mug—comforting, soothing, and redolent of autumn. It's the perfect drink to serve your leaf-raking crew when they hit your doorstep, ready for refreshment. Add a shot of bourbon for extra warming power. MAKES 1 DRINK

---

2 tablespoons Boiled Apple Syrup (page 64)

1½ tablespoons Spiced Maple Syrup (page 68)

1 cup boiling water

Put both of the syrups in a large mug. Fill to the top with the boiling water, stir well, and serve.

HOT APPLE TODDY

Any type of toddy is a cool-weather cup of warm cheer, but this one is especially warming with its wintry spice mix married with the round, wine-like fragrance of the apple reduction. The vanilla-and-wood tones of the bourbon add to its complexity and flavor—a serious modern take on your grandmother's nightcap. MAKES 1 DRINK

2 tablespoons bourbon

2 tablespoons Boiled Apple Syrup (page 64)

1 tablespoon Spiced Maple Syrup (page 68)

1 cup boiling water

Cinnamon stick, for garnish

Lemon wheel, for garnish

Combine the bourbon and syrups in a mug, then top with the boiling water. Garnish with the cinnamon stick and lemon wheel, and serve.

ACKNOWLEDGMENTS

It's been a wild ride since I started P&H Soda Co. I wouldn't have made it this far without the support of my wife, Erica. She is the main reason why I started the company and why it still exists today. She continues to stand by my side through thick and thin.

I would like to thank my family and friends for all of the support they have given me. To my mom and dad: Lana, Rick, and Richie. To my brothers and sisters: Jason, AJ, Adam, Tony, Selina, Tiluna, Lumia, and Marco. Also, thanks to my friends Virgil Bastos, Tia Keenan, and Shamus Jones for their constant moral support.

I'm very grateful to the people who gave me a chance and helped my company get to where it is today. Harry Rosenblum and Taylor Erkkinen at The Brooklyn Kitchen were my first account and gave me a chance to sell my syrups at their wonderful store. Joann Kim invited me to sell my very first soda at the Greenpoint Food Market. Thanks to all of the New York City–based food producers who make this city one of the best in the world for new and exciting handcrafted products.

Thank you to the many people who have written or videotaped stories about P&H Soda Co. for blogs, magazines, and newspapers.

My writer, Lynn Marie Hulsman, and my agent, Sharon Bowers, thank you for all of the hard work and support you have put into this book. Lynn did a wonderful job of putting my thoughts into words, and Sharon was always there when I needed her.

Thanks to my editor, Ashley Phillips, and the staff at Clarkson Potter for convincing me to write this book.

My photographer, Alexandra Grablewski, and prop stylist, Genna Moss, thank you for amazing days of shooting. Everything looks great!

Chris Gray and Beth Lewand at Eastern District and Ica Morales, thanks for being my taste test guinea pigs.

Thanks to Darcy O'Neil for writing *Fix the Pumps*. His research and understanding of the classic soda fountain are invaluable and have taught us a lot.

Most important, I want to thank all of the customers who have purchased my soda, my syrups, and this book. Without you, I would not exist as the person I am today.

Thank you all for your continued support!

SOURCES

ART OF DRINK
www.artofdrink.com

A great place to buy bottles of acid phosphate and lactart. You'll also find Darcy O'Neil's excellent book *Fix the Pumps*, chronicling the history of the soda fountain, as well as drinks and techniques used by early soda jerks.

1673 Richmond Street, Suite No. 513
London, Ontario
Canada N5Y 1R1
dso@artofdrink.com

AMAZON
www.amazon.com

Amazon sells nearly everything you'll need for soda making, barring fresh ingredients: coconut sugar, chocolate husks (listed as organic chocolate tea, but containing 100 percent food-grade cocoa husks), chicory, citric acid (sour salt), caster sugar, maple sugar, and organic sugar.

800-201-7575

THE BROOKLYN KITCHEN
www.thebrooklynkitchen.com

A great place to buy coffee and tea, as well as cool kitchen items, from coupes to canning jars. They also offer classes on pig butchering, pickling, and, of course, soda making.

100 Frost Street
Brooklyn, NY 11211
718-389-2982

COMMUNITY COFFEE COMPANY
www.communitycoffee.com

The perfect source for the pure chicory they use in their famous coffee blends.

P.O. Box 2311
Baton Rouge, LA 70821
800-643-8199

KALUSTYAN'S
www.kalustyans.com

An unparalleled supplier of spices and Middle Eastern and Indian ingredients. If you need something exotic or obscure, check here.

123 Lexington Avenue
New York, NY 10016
800-352-3451

MOUNTAIN ROSE HERBS
www.mountainroseherbs.com

Mountain Rose sells dried burdock root, lavender flowers, rose petals, star anise, and many other herbs and botanicals used in soda making.

P.O. Box 50220
Eugene, OR 97405
800-879-3337

SERENDIPITEA
www.serendipitea.com

SerendipiTea is one of my favorite purveyors of botanicals, herbs, and spices. Look for dried flowers, dried fruits, and star anise.

73 Plandome Road
Manhasset, NY 11030
888-832-5433

WINE FOREST WILD FOODS
www.wineforest.com

A fellow Good Food Awards winner, Wine Forest Wild Foods supplies top-quality wild and tamed foods to discerning wholesale and retail customers. You'll find exotic offerings like fennel pollen rub, porcini powder, and candy cap mushrooms.

6493 Dry Creek Road
Napa, CA 94558
707-944-8604

INDEX